One-Pot Wonders

For Kristina (whhat)

James Barber

James Barber

One-Pot Wonders

James Barber's Recipes for Land and Sea

HARBOUR PUBLISHING

Harbour Publishing Co. Ltd.
P.O. Box 219
Madeira Park, BC
V0N 2H0
www.harbourpublishing.com

Design by A. Comfort
Cover illustration by Kim LaFave
Text illustrations by Kim LaFave and James Barber
Printed and bound in Canada

Harbour Publishing acknowledges financial support from the Government of Canada through the Book Publishing Industry Development Program and the Canada Council for the Arts, and from the Province of British Columbia through the British Columbia Arts Council and the Book Publisher's Tax Credit through the Ministry of Provincial Revenue.

Library and Archives Canada Cataloguing in Publication

Barber, James, 1923-
   One-pot wonders : James Barber's recipes for land and sea / James Barber.

Includes index.

ISBN 1-55017-378-2

   1. One-dish meals. I. Title.
TX840.O53B37 2006   641.8'2   C2006-900289-4

DEDICATION

To all Cal 20 owners, past, present, future and just looking.

CONTENTS

ACKNOWLEDGEMENTS   VIII

THE ONE-POT COOK   1

GALLEY ESSENTIALS   2

1 – APPETIZERS   7

2 – SALADS   17

3 – EGGS   31

4 – MEAT AND POULTRY   39

5 – FRESH SEAFOOD   55

6 – SALMON ON THE SHELF   66

7 – BARBECUE   71

8 – PASTA AND NOODLES   83

9 – RICE   100

10 – DESSERTS   105

11 – ONE-POT CHRISTMAS   115

INDEX   118

ACKNOWLEDGEMENTS

Thanks for the enthusiasm Peter Robson, Wendy Bone, and Mary Schendlinger

THE ONE-POT COOK

One-pot dinners are the simplest survival kits. Once you learn the technique, you can get by anywhere in the world. The rich, the poor, kids, dogs, beautiful women and handsome men, boat owners and even people with butlers and Ferraris, they'll all invite you for weekends, they'll take you to their pleasure palaces, on their boats, even on the backs of their motorbikes. They'll sleep with you, buy you diamonds, fly you to Mozambique (or Minnesota), marry you, even stop smoking for you. One-pot cooks are lovable, desirable and affordable people to live with. Just ask any one of them, or better still, learn how and see for yourself.

You don't need a Cordon Bleu certificate or a library of cookbooks to be a good cook, but you do need some sort of stove. I've cooked food with a blowtorch, made soup with the steamer on a cappuccino machine, improvised ovens from used oil drums and baked cakes on a barbecue. You also need half a dozen or so basic techniques—ways of cooking that bring you an understanding of what you're doing. You need a sharp knife and a decent pot with a lid, but most of all you need self-confidence to just get on and do it. Most cooking shows and cookbooks are very good at making you feel insecure.

The recipes in this book are for dishes that can be made in one pot (or pan). Okay, a few are not strictly one-pot, but they're all do-able with a minimum of space and equipment, in a one-burner boat galley, bachelor apartment, RV, campsite, and (best of all) in the strange kitchens of people you just happen to meet and just happen to find yourself waking up with next morning.

GALLEY ESSENTIALS

equipment

Noisy, stinky, no sleep and terrible food—the worst job I ever had was on a seiner out of Bellingham. The skipper drank Jack Daniel's straight from the bottle and the rest of us stayed sober to stay alive. We fished on shares—no fish, no money—and for a month there was nothing, But one night my share was $3,000, and I quit. Never again. Looking back, I blame the whole bad trip on an enormous black fry pan that seemed to be the only equipment in the galley. We all used it when we needed to eat (there was no cook). The rule was never wash it, so eggs, steak, bacon and sausages went in and came out of it blacker and greasier than a summer's-end barbecue. Three quarters of a million dollars worth of boat, almost half of that in very expensive electronics, and the galley with this stinking archaic piece of equipment.

Since then I've been on a lot of fishboats, and that black iron fry pan seems to be a macho badge of honour, a determined holdout against "the wife" and her "fancy ideas." I've taken to leaving a non-stick pan behind as a boat gift, and most of them are still being used when I go back ("Next thing you'll be giving me an apron ... "). It seems that about 50 percent of boat owners tend to skimp on the galley, while the other half clutter it up with enough rubbishy gimmicks to stock an all-day garage sale.

You need a big pot (about 5 qts/5 L), a 12" [30 cm] fry pan with a lid that fits both it and the pot, and a smaller saucepan for eggs and hot drinks. I buy mine from Paderno—heavy stainless steel, easy to clean, Canadian-made on Prince Edward Island, inexpensive and virtually indestructible, and the handles stay cool. I use them at home, in the cooking school, on the boat and on the beach. They make great stewpots, great bailers and great oil-draining pans, and you can get a large crab in the big pot. Which is also big enough to do dishes in, or bath the cat ...

You need a couple of sharp knives, a paring knife and an 8" [20 cm] chef's knife. You also need a good two-sided cutting board, a stainless-steel grater, a wooden spoon and a spatula for getting things out of the fry pan. I like the Zyliss potato peeler, which also makes fancy strips of carrot or orange peel if you want to tart up a salad or grate cheese for pasta. A strainer of some sort is handy, and two or three plastic snap-top containers, a packet of zip-lock bags and a couple of stainless steel mixing bowls. And that's about it. Two forks held in one hand make a very efficient egg whisk. You'll need a corkscrew (although you can push the cork into the bottle with a chopstick), but you don't need brandy snifters or asparagus cookers or fancy egg poachers. It's easier to modify your cooking habits than spend your life first longing for fancy equipment and then looking for a place to stow it. There may be a PhD thesis in this as an explanation for two foot-itis.

The one thing you must never do is keep sharp knives in drawers, where they will almost immediately become blunt and useless.

ingredients

The only thing I'm really fussy about is oil—canola or peanut to cook with and a small bottle of really good olive oil, which will turn the dreariest of vegetables (cooked or raw) into a super salad. Don't leave a large bottle of olive oil on the boat in summer—it goes rancid very quickly—and don't buy cheap olive oil. You can use grape-seed oil in the fry pan (it has a high smoking point).

Hard-line gourmets will have heart attacks if you mention stock cubes, but a packet of the best you can find (without MSG) will do a great deal to enrich whatever you serve. Asian stores sell Dashi powder (to make the stock that is the basis of most Japanese cooking), and again, look for one that has no MSG. Keep them in a screw-top jar, tightly sealed.

And cans. Canned tomatoes are better than winter tomatoes, canned corn is fine in breakfast pancakes and fritters, canned clams make a quick pasta sauce, canned salmon is a godsend for fishcakes, canned consommé laced with a bit of sherry is a marvel on a cold winter day. Cans will save your reputation, but you need a decent can opener—a cheap one is a waste of time.

Rice is better on boats than pasta (it doesn't need an extra pot to cook in), brown sugar keeps best in a screw-top jar and is less messy than honey, and peanut butter is a seriously under-appreciated ingredient in one-pot dishes (more on that later). A couple of lemons, a piece of ginger and a bottle of soy sauce also keep well without rotting. If one pot is what you're striving for, quick, simple and flavourful are the key words.

herbs and spices

The best spice (and the best tool) on a boat is the willingness to improvise, to use what you've got. Cookbooks have to be specific, otherwise they'd go on and on for pages and pages offering alternatives and substitutions—"If you don't have this, use that." But cooking doesn't have to be rigid. It's like painting a picture or making love—you use what's there and the end result has the special flavour of you in it. Everybody has a grandma who makes something special and nobody in the family can reproduce it exactly the way she does, because she has her own system of measuring and thinking about food. Recipes are just guidelines or rough maps pointing to dinner, and dinners are like love affairs, never the same twice running. The secret to being a good cook is fine-tuning the recipes you remember liking, and learning to make the best of what you've got. Again (and don't ever forget it), like love affairs.

I watch the worriers pushing their carts around the supermarket, long list (or Palm Pilot) in hand, dinner next Friday and this is only Monday, desperately looking for frog's legs, size 7½ AAA, or Old Mother Wilson's homestyle bean flavouring, or fresh Indonesian black peppercorns. Come Friday they're exhausted and dinner is a chore. If you're on a boat or in a small apartment, there just isn't room for an A to Z of spices, three different varieties of salt and a library of stocks. You have to learn to make do, particularly with herbs and spices, none of which keep well in large quantities or on boats. So you put small quantities in small jars or film canisters, throw them out regularly and refill.

And you don't need dozens of flavourings. Salt and pepper are essential. So are red pepper flakes and curry powder. Fresh ginger root is something you'll soon learn never to be without, and a weird little star-shaped spice called star anise. All of them are available in supermarkets. A little tin of dry mustard is nice, and after that you need one sweet herb and one pungent one. Tarragon, basil and mint are interchangeable for the sweet, and thyme, oregano and rosemary for the pungent. Use what you've got, and be generous with them all, except salt.

dressings

Don't clutter your galley with bottles of store-bought dressings. It's cheaper and quicker to make your own. Pour about ½" [1 cm] of oil into an empty screw-top spice jar and carefully pour in vinegar (or alternatives; see p. 18), which will sink to the bottom. When there's three times as much oil as vinegar, add a pinch of salt and whatever herb you fancy, put the lid on, shake well and there you are—salad dressing. If you want an eggy mayonnaise, crack an egg into this dressing, add a pinch of mustard and shake vigorously. Bingo, you're cooking. It's not Julia Child, but it's good—on cold chicken or fish or on egg salad, chicken or ham sandwiches. Just don't forget you're on a boat.

1 – APPETIZERS

You only need appetizers if dinner is going to be late and people want something to eat while they're waiting, or you want a little party for sailpast, or your in-laws threaten to visit. There are a few easy things that you can conjure up in a small galley with a minimum of fuss, that will glamorize the simplest of suppers.

baked olives

1 cup [250 mL] black oil-cured
   olives from the deli
   (not canned olives)
1 clove garlic, chopped
1 Tbsp [15 mL] olive oil
¼ cup [60 mL] white wine

Put everything in a fry pan, cover and cook 5 minutes over medium heat. Put the olives in a dish and be surprised at how pleased your guests are.

russian egg salad

In Queen Victoria's day, when it was fashionable to have a few anglicized French items on the menus of the English court, lots of simple, essentially British dishes were re-christened. Good old egg salad, an essential Sunday tea item, became Oeufs à la Russe—*or, for those who found that name a bit too foreign, Russian Egg Salad.*

handful of walnuts
1 Tbsp [15 mL] olive oil
3 sprinkles of salt
sprinkle of dill (dried is fine
    unless you've got fresh
    growing on the foredeck)
2 hard-boiled eggs, peeled and
    chopped into eighths
2 Tbsp [30 mL] hot pepper
    relish *or* salsa

Chop the walnuts coarse and fry them in the oil 5 minutes over medium-low heat. Sprinkle with salt and dill, let cool 5 minutes, pour over eggs and then pour relish over everything. Serve it with crackers, veggies, anything crisp enough to hold it.

potatoes with walnuts and yogurt

2 potatoes, cut into bite-sized pieces
handful of walnuts
1 Tbsp [15 mL] olive oil
½ cup [125 mL] yogurt
few sprigs of cilantro *or* **parsley, chopped**
salt and pepper

Put the potatoes in a pot, cover them with water, bring to the boil and cook 12–15 minutes over medium heat. Meanwhile, toast the walnuts in a dry fry pan for 2 minutes over high heat (or have someone else do it). Cool the walnuts, then chop them. When the potatoes are done, drain them and toss immediately with the walnuts, oil, yogurt and cilantro. Season to taste with salt and pepper.

garlic mushrooms

2 Tbsp [30 mL] butter
1 lb [450 g] small white
    mushrooms *or* large
    ones, quartered
2 cloves garlic, chopped fine
juice of half a lemon
chopped parsley for garnish
salt and pepper

Melt the butter in a fry pan over medium heat, add the mushrooms and garlic, and cook 5 minutes, stirring occasionally. Stir in the lemon juice and cook 3 minutes. Sprinkle with parsley, season to taste with salt and pepper, and serve.

clams daniel

1 Tbsp [15 mL] olive oil
1 medium onion, chopped fine
1 clove garlic, chopped fine
½ tsp [2 mL] curry powder
1 tsp [5 mL] pepper
juice of half a lemon
1 can [7 oz/200 mL] baby clams
1 Tbsp [15 mL] sherry
chopped parsley for garnish

Heat the oil in a fry pan over medium heat, and fry the onion and garlic until transparent. Add curry powder and pepper and stir well. Drain the clams, reserving the clam juice for the cooks to drink with vodka. Add lemon juice, clams and sherry to the pan. Cook 2 minutes, sprinkle with parsley and let people shovel it up on tortilla chips.

mushrooms and mint

8 oz [225 g] small white
    mushrooms
1 tsp [5 mL] salt
1 tsp [5 mL] dried *or*
    chopped fresh mint
juice of 1 lemon
chopped parsley for garnish

Put everything in a jar with a lid and shake gently so that the juices coat the mushrooms. Let sit for 15 minutes, tip out and eat with toothpicks or fingers. Bright and very refreshing.

mushrooms and mint and tuna

1 can [7½ oz/213 g] tuna
8 oz [225 g] small white
    mushrooms
½ tsp [2 mL] salt
big handful green *or* black olives
2 Tbsp [30 mL] olive oil
1 tsp [5 mL] dried *or*
    chopped fresh mint
½ tsp [2 mL] black pepper
1 bunch green onions, sliced
    into thin rings

Break up tuna and mix it in a bowl with everything else *except* the onion. Let marinate 15 minutes, sprinkle with onion and serve with pita bread or crackers.

chickpea vinaigrette

1 can [15 oz/425 mL] chickpeas,
    washed and drained
juice of 1 medium orange
1 Tbsp [15 mL] olive oil
chopped parsley for garnish
1 tsp [5 mL] salt
½ tsp [2 mL] pepper

Mix all ingredients together and serve with pita bread cut into triangles.

spiced peanuts

1 lb [450 g] dry-roasted peanuts
1 Tbsp [15 mL] olive oil
1 tsp [5 mL] curry powder
½ tsp [2 mL] salt

Heat peanuts in a dry fry pan over medium heat. Add oil and curry powder, stir well and cook 2 minutes. Tip out onto a paper towel and sprinkle with salt.

2 – SALADS

Leafy vegetables are not easy to keep on boats. I favour the crisp ones—fennel, Belgian endive, romaine lettuce hearts, cabbage and celery, which will stay in reasonable shape for most of a week. Green beans are good keepers if they're fresh when you buy them (no brown spots), mushrooms keep well in a paper bag, apples keep but pears don't. I always have a bag of almonds or walnuts, which, heated up in a fry pan until light brown, do wonders for the blandest of salads. Sweet peppers keep well if they don't get too much rolling about and bruising, and tomatoes (so long as they're not the pallid pink winter cheapos) make a very good simple salad with nothing more than oil and salt. A small bottle of Chinese sesame oil is a good thing to have around to give variety to your salad dressings.

basic salad dressing

You need an empty spice jar or other small screw-top jar. Pour in about ½" [1 cm] of olive oil, then carefully pour in vinegar until you have exactly three times as much oil as vinegar. The oil will float, so you can see when to stop. Add a pinch or two of salt and pepper to taste, screw the top on and shake well.

Substitutes for olive oil: Sesame oil, walnut oil, hazelnut oil, grape-seed oil.

Substitutes for vinegar: Lemon juice, orange juice, balsamic vinegar, good beer.

Additions: Sesame seeds, thyme, rosemary, tarragon.

Variations: Add a whole egg to the basic and shake well for something close to runny mayonnaise. Add 1 Tbsp [15 mL] plain yogurt to the basic with herbs as a dressing for chickpeas. Add 1 tsp [5 mL] tomato paste to the basic and serve over cold leftover pasta.

fennel salad
Serves 4

1 fennel bulb
1 Tbsp [15 mL] olive oil
salt and pepper
juice of ½ orange

Cut the fennel root lengthwise in quarters, then slice crosswise as thin as you can. Toss with olive oil, salt and pepper (no vinegar) and squeeze the orange juice over top. Toss, let sit 10 minutes and eat after your main course.

hot bacon salad

Serves 2–4

A quick, filling supper with a loaf of good bread and enough vitamins to keep scurvy at bay for a whole weekend. On its own there's lots for two, with some left over for bubble and squeak next day, and as a side dish for meat (like a barbecued flank steak) it's more than adequate for four.

8 oz [225 g] sliced bacon
1 head romaine
1 bunch green onions, cut
    into ½" [1 cm] lengths
2 Tbsp [30 mL] vinegar
½ tsp [2 mL] sugar
pepper
salt

Cut the bacon crosswise into ½" [1 cm] strips and cook in a dry fry pan over medium heat until crisp. This will take 10 minutes or so— 10 minutes that will make everybody on-board very hungry and anxious to help. Let them remove the coarse outside leaves from the romaine (keep in a plastic bag for tomorrow's soup), then cut the romaine lengthwise into quarters. Slice the quarters crosswise into 1" [2.5 cm] pieces, separate the leaves a bit and put them in a heatproof bowl. Drain the bacon on a paper towel. Pour most of the fat from the pan (leave 3 or 4 Tbsp/40–50 mL), turn heat to high and stir-fry the green onion 1 minute. Stir in the vinegar, sugar and pepper to taste, and cook 30 seconds. Add the bacon to the greens and pour the cooked dressing over all. Toss well, add salt to taste (some bacon is saltier than others) and eat immediately with good bread and good beer.

You can use spinach, cabbage or savoy cabbage sliced thin instead of lettuce, but you'll be disappointed if you use iceberg lettuce, which doesn't have enough body to give the salad its essential crispness.

cabbage salad
Serves 4

½ green cabbage
1 medium brown onion
1 clove garlic
2 Tbsp [30 mL] olive oil
10 thin slices fresh ginger
1 small packet salted peanuts
4 oz [115 g] golden raisins *or*
    sultanas *or* chopped figs,
      dates, apple *or* a combination
½ cup [125 mL] beer *or* apple juice

Cut the cabbage in half, remove the hard core and slice crosswise very thin. Thin-slice the onion and crush the garlic. Heat the oil in a fry pan over medium heat. Add the garlic, ginger and peanuts and cook 30 seconds. Add the fruit and cook 30 seconds longer. Add the cabbage, turn the heat up to high, toss well, add the beer, cover and cook 3 minutes. Good hot or cold.

Some people add a few anchovies with the garlic. Some people add cubed ham, and some add 1 tsp [5 mL] sesame oil at the last moment. And some people add a can of red salmon (7½ oz/213 g) for the last 3 minutes, which turns it into a lot of salad. Leftovers make a good soup next day cooked with a bit of water (or beer or white wine or chicken stock).

hot salad of sweet peppers

Serves 4

You can eat this salad hot or cold with meat, fish or chicken, or make it part of a cold Mediterranean lunch next day. The anchovies literally melt—nobody can see them, but everybody will comment on the bright, sweet-sour flavour of the sauce that sticks to the peppers.

**2 or 3 shiny sweet red and
    yellow peppers**
2 Tbsp [30 mL] olive oil
1 clove garlic, chopped
½ tsp [2 mL] salt
3 anchovy fillets
2 Tbsp [30 mL] vinegar
½ tsp [2 mL] sugar

Seed the peppers and cut into 1" (2.5 cm) squares (more or less). Heat the oil in a fry pan over medium-high heat and fry the garlic 30 seconds. Add the sweet peppers and the salt. Cook 2 minutes, turning to coat everything with oil. Add anchovies and cook 2 minutes, turning so the anchovies can melt. Add the vinegar, sprinkle with sugar and toss well for 1 minute.

warm mushroom salad with green beans
Serves 4

2 Tbsp [30 mL] olive oil
8 oz [225 g] skinny green beans
   or skinny asparagus, cut
   into 1" [2.5 cm] lengths
½ tsp each salt and pepper
8 oz [225 g] white
   mushrooms, halved
½ tsp [2 mL] dried mint
juice of half a lemon

Heat the oil in a fry pan over high heat. Add the beans, sprinkle with salt (keeps them green) and cook 1 minute. Add the mushrooms and stir well. Turn the heat to low, add the mint and lemon juice, cover and cook 2 minutes.

fagioli fiorentina

Serves 4
Very easy.

1 can [15 oz/425 mL] white beans,
    well rinsed and drained
1 medium onion, chopped fine
1 tsp [5 mL] pepper
½ tsp [2 mL] dried
    oregano *or* thyme
3 Tbsp [40 mL] olive oil
juice of 1 lemon *or* half an orange
½ bunch parsley, chopped
1 can [7½ oz/213 g] tuna,
    broken up

Mix everything together well with a fork and let sit 15 minutes. The more parsley, the better.

peanut butter salad

Thin 2 Tbsp [30 mL] Super All-Purpose Peanut Sauce (p. 28) with lemon juice, orange juice or sherry until it's the consistency of mayonnaise. Add a pinch of salt or 1 tsp [5 mL] soy sauce.

Toss the dressing with a salad of fine-cut vegetables (lettuce, cabbage, diced apple or red pepper, fine-diced carrot) for two. Toss in some cold cubed tofu (or ham or crisp fried bacon) and sprinkle with freshly ground pepper and chopped green onion.

peanut butter

Every time I go to France, I take a 5-gallon [20 L] pail of peanut butter. Customs officers wave me through, after raising their eyebrows and their shoulders, then rolling their eyes in that uniquely French way that says, wordlessly and effectively, that there is no point in trying to understand anybody who isn't French.

Peanut butter isn't illegal in France, but it certainly isn't *cuisine française*. Despite being enormously popular, it's almost impossible to find in Paris and even harder to come by in the country. My pail is always empty in a couple of days. The Citroëns and the Renaults start to arrive within minutes and people happily trade a couple of bottles of good wine or some expensive *foie gras* for a dollar's worth, which they take home and eat—like 90 percent of North American kids—with bananas in sandwiches.

Peanut butter just doesn't seem to turn up as a main ingredient in cookbook indexes. You'll find recipes for peanut sauce that involve tracking down fresh Louisiana peanuts (medium large) and spending three hours blanching, drying, roasting, skinning and finally grinding them to produce something archly called "the paste," but you won't often find the simple instruction "take 2 heaping Tbsp peanut butter." Which is a shame, because a jar of crunchy peanut butter can turn the simplest ingredients into kid-friendly, visitor-impressing and, most important, quick-and-easy-on-the-cook dishes of the kind that I call "almost gourmet." For example, if you serve peanut butter with a big plate of cut-up vegetables (cauliflower, sweet peppers, carrots, green onions, whatever's fresh and colourful), and chunks of good crusty country bread, or pita or tortilla chips, and you encourage people to be gluttonous, kids will suddenly begin to like vegetables. There are hundreds of other simple recipes that call for peanut butter. Just make sure you buy the best you can, with "100 percent peanuts" on the label.

super all-purpose peanut sauce

Makes about 2 cups [500 mL]

Having convinced yourself that peanut butter is okay, it's time to move on to an all-purpose peanut sauce, which will keep in the fridge for a month and transform almost any food into something really exotic.

1 can [14 oz/398 mL] coconut milk
¼ cup [60 mL] chunky
    peanut butter
1" [2.5 cm] piece fresh
    ginger, chopped fine
3 cloves garlic, chopped
4 red chili peppers, chopped,
    or 1 tsp [5 mL] hot sauce
juice of 1 lemon
¼ cup [60 mL] water, *or* beer
    or even Coca Cola
2 Tbsp [30 mL] brown sugar
2 Tbsp [30 mL] sesame oil

Whizz it all smooth in a food processor or blender and keep covered in the fridge. The sauce will thicken, but it thins out as it warms up.

Spread it on anything barbecued—hamburgers, small cubes of chicken on sticks, fish, pork chops, tofu, those skinny little Japanese eggplants, grilled tomatoes, corn, fish. Mix it with lightly steamed vegetables (broccoli, green beans, cauliflower, baby squash), or dilute it a bit with water, lemon juice or a little sherry, and toss it with salad greens. Thai and Vietnamese cooks add fish sauce to the basic mixture, others add curry paste, but the essential flavour is peanuts, garlic, a little hot and spicy, a little bright with the lemon juice.

basic quick peanut sauce
Makes about ¼ cup [60 mL]
A simpler version of the Super Sauce.

1 heaping Tbsp [20 mL]
    peanut butter
juice of 1 lemon
½ tsp [2 mL] red pepper flakes
2 Tbsp [30 mL] beer, *or* water
    or wine or whisky

Mix together peanut butter, the lemon juice and red pepper flakes. As you mix, the sauce will go stiff. Now thin it out by stirring in beer, or water or wine or whisky. This is the basic last-three-days sauce for just about anything—chicken, fish, vegetables, or just spread it on bread.

peanut butter for special occasions

You're tied up at Otter Bay in your Cal 20 when the wife of the skipper of the 65-footer on the outside float comes over to tell you that she remembers when her husband had a little boat like this and it was so cramped, so would you like to come over for drinks and dinner? "Nothing formal, just a few people ... six-ish ..." You feel you have to take something, so one of you nips up the dock to buy whatever vegetables haven't totally wilted (broccoli, carrots, radishes, green onions, a cucumber—whatever you can find), a loaf of bread and a pot of yogurt (plain is best, but if there's only raspberry, take that). Meanwhile, the other half makes a double portion of Basic Quick Peanut Sauce, which you mix with an equal quantity of yogurt (stir it well). Cut the vegetables and bread into bite-sized pieces and arrange them around the bowl of modified sauce. This is also a great emergency quick party food at home, and a good way to persuade kids to eat their vegetables.

Whatever you do, don't buy cheap peanut butter with sugar in it. Read the label, and pay a bit more.

peanut butter for barbecues

Add a pinch of sugar to Super All-Purpose Peanut Sauce and spread it on top of a hamburger for the last half of the cooking (not on the underside, because it will burn). Do the same with pork or lamb chops. Sprinkle with lemon juice before eating.

3 – EGGS

Doing nothing on a boat is almost impossible and takes a lot of determination. Forget the varnishing, the polishing, the cleaning out of lockers, the splicing and the rest of the job list. Decide to do nothing at all—just sit and relax, turn off the cellphone and the radio and let yourself melt into the special motion of a boat going nowhere. A couple of beers, a bottle of gin, a book or some Mozart, it's a psychic massage, the purest of self-indulgences.

But you have to eat. And the doing nothing includes cooking. Or rather not cooking. Which brings us to Tortilla Españole. Italians call their version frittata, the North American approximation is Denver omelette and the Japanese edition is okonomi. They're all slightly different and all very much the same—dead easy, comforting and filling. You can make it at home for lunch boxes or on the boat for a quick supper. You can eat it cold or hot, or you can cut it into elegant wedges and have a quick party. I like to take it down to the boat and eat it all. Just me.

tortilla españole
Serves 4

1 large potato, cut in dice a bit
smaller than sugar cubes
1 medium onion, cut
in smaller dice
3 Tbsp [45 mL] olive oil
6 eggs
1 tsp [5 mL] salt
½ tsp [2 mL] pepper
dried thyme *or* rosemary *or*
red pepper flakes to taste

Heat the oil in a fry pan over medium heat and cook the potato and onion, stirring occasionally, for 10 minutes or until the potato is just tender. Beat the eggs with the salt, pepper and thyme. Pour the eggs over the potatoes, turn the heat to low, cover the pan with a lid or a plate and cook about 10 minutes until the top is just firm. Lay a plate face-down over the pan, hold it firm and flip the pan over so that the nice brown side is up. Slide the tortilla back into the pan, cook 2 minutes and that's it. Let it cool a bit in the pan and eat it hot or cold. Great party food, and it will keep a couple of days in the icebox.

When you've made it once, try again. Use fresh (even frozen) asparagus instead of the potatoes, or green beans. Add chopped garlic sausage if you have it, or a bit of chopped ham. You can add bits (not too much) of almost any vegetable chopped small, or crisp chopped bacon, and frozen peas are fine if you shake them out of the packet and let them defrost for 5 minutes before cooking. Chutney from a jar goes well with Tortilla Españole, and so do good bread and red wine. The only art is in flipping it, but be bold and suddenly you'll know how.

huevos rancheros, boat style

Serves 2

It's the simplest one-pot supper I know, and my favourite breakfast, lunch or dinner—eggs on a boat. Tomatoes are good for a couple of months every year, juicy and succulent and (on a boat) very squashable. The rest of the year they're pallid and flavourless. Most recipes for Huevos Rancheros give you fussy directions to peel and seed tomatoes. There's nothing wrong with that if you've nothing else to do, if you're not hungry and if you're anywhere else but on a boat. But you are on a boat, and you don't want to be doing dishes. You want shortcuts. There's nothing wrong with canned tomatoes—Italians use them most of the time, they're picked at their ripest and juiciest, and a can of diced tomatoes contains less juice and twice as much flesh as you'll get out of a pound of tomatoes mucked about à la Martha Stewart. Most recipes will also tell you to lightly fry the onion, then lightly fry the garlic (taking care not to brown or burn them), both of which take time that you can use for another purpose—like watching the moon rise, since you are on a boat. Onions need pre-cooking to develop their best taste in sauces, but Italian cooks have a procedure they call battuto *that is no-fuss and burn-proof. I know this is a Mexican recipe, but Italians are the masters of quick cooking so why not use it?*

2 Tbsp [30 mL] peanut oil *or* grape-seed oil
1 medium onion, chopped coarse
2 cloves garlic, chopped
½ tsp [2 mL] red pepper flakes *or* 1 tsp [5 mL] hot paprika
1 tsp [5 mL] dried thyme *or* oregano

1 tsp [5 mL] dried mint
1 can [14 oz/398 mL]
    diced tomatoes
4 large eggs
salt and pepper

Put the onion and garlic in a fry pan with the oil and ¼ cup [60 mL] water, bring to the boil and simmer 2–3 minutes until the water is almost gone (that's the *battuto*). Add the chili pepper and thyme and stir 2 seconds. Add the mint and tomatoes and bring to a quick boil, while you crack the eggs into a saucer. Cook the sauce 5 minutes, slide the eggs on top of the sauce, sprinkle with salt and pepper, cover and cook over medium heat until the eggs are ready (traditionally the yolks should still be runny). Slide out of the pan and eat immediately with good bread and cheap red wine.

Serve with tortillas or bread or, if you're really hungry, a can of white beans. Rinse the beans well and heat them for 2 minutes with 3 Tbsp [45 mL] water, in the pan (not washed) that you cooked the Huevos Rancheros in.

Variations: Add 1 tsp [5 mL] cumin seeds or a bit of orange zest to the *battuto* before cooking, and/or add 1 Tbsp [15 mL] tomato paste to the tomatoes. I have friends who make the ranchero sauce, then put halved hard-boiled eggs in it, and others who pour the sauce over spaghetti. Your boat, your choice.

some other things to do with eggs

omelette

Serves 2

The quickest meal in any kitchen is an omelette—with practice you can turn out one a minute. The trick to a good omelette is keeping it light. And the secrets to that are first, don't put milk in it; second, have a hot enough pan; and third, use 3 eggs. A one-egg omelette gets tough, and 4 eggs or more get burnt on the bottom.

3 eggs
pinch of salt
pinch of red pepper flakes
water
1 Tbsp [15 mL] oil *or* butter

Heat the pan on medium heat. Crack eggs into a bowl, and add salt and red pepper flakes. Fill half an eggshell with water and add that to the eggs. Beat very lightly with a fork, leaving some white and some yellow. When the pan is hot, put in oil or butter, and wave the pan about over the burner until the bottom is covered. Immediately pour in the eggs and stir them with the fork held flat and the tines pointing up, lifting the cooked eggs from the bottom to the top. When the eggs look shiny and still a bit liquid, fold over a third of the omelette in the pan, then flip the covered bit over the rest and tip on to a plate. The omelette will continue to cook on the plate. Any fool can overcook an omelette.

scrambled eggs à deux

Serves 2

This is a great lunch for two with a green salad, and lovely with a couple of slices of smoked salmon on top.

4 eggs
½ tsp [2 mL] salt
pinch of pepper
pinch of thyme
¼ cup [60 mL] milk
2 Tbsp [30 mL] butter
chopped parsley *or* thin-
    sliced green onion

Beat together eggs, salt, a good pinch of pepper, a big pinch of thyme and milk. Cook over medium-low heat with butter, stirring slowly to make large curds. Sprinkle with parsley. Don't overcook. The eggs should come off the heat while the tops are still moist.

eggs benedict with variations

Serves 2

Make this with any vegetable, fresh or frozen—green beans, broccoli, spinach, green peas ...

2 Tbsp [30 mL] olive oil
vegetables for 2, cut in bite-
     sized pieces (break
     them up if frozen)
3 Tbsp [45 mL] water
4 eggs
salt and pepper

Heat a fry pan over medium heat. Add the oil, then add the vegetables and sprinkle with salt to taste. Toss to coat well with oil, add the water, cover and cook 3 minutes. Meanwhile, crack the eggs into a saucer. Slide them onto the vegetables, sprinkle with salt and pepper to taste, cover and cook 3–4 minutes until the eggs are just cooked (take the lid off and check at 3 minutes). Eat immediately.

Variations: Sprinkle a few drops of sesame oil over the eggs just before serving.

Shred half a green cabbage and toss in melted butter in a pan for 2 minutes, then pour the eggs on top, cover and cook 3–4 minutes. Cabbage needs a bit more salt and pepper, or add soy sauce instead of salt.

eggs au naturel

If you can't be bothered with any of the previous recipes, there's nothing better than half a dozen hard-boiled eggs, a good loaf of bread, some salt and a six-pack.

Everybody knows how to boil an egg, but very few know the secret of doing it well. Put the eggs (up to a dozen) in a saucepan, cover by 1" [2.5 cm] with cold water, bring to the boil and turn off the heat. Then let them sit in the water to cool for 15 minutes. They'll be perfectly cooked, easier to peel and less granular to the taste, and they won't have that black line around the yolk. Put them back in the egg box and you have ready-to-go quick lunches.

Hard-boiled eggs go very well tossed in a cabbage salad with lots of salt and chopped onion. Or cut them into chunks and mix them with slightly larger chunks of cold cooked potato, sprinkle with chopped parsley, olive oil, a dash of vinegar and a lot of pepper, and you have an instant potato salad that's a great improvement on the usual picnic offering.

And for the someone who won't leave the wheel ("Just let me get us through Porlier ... "), two peeled boiled eggs (one at a time) and a cold beer are ideal, especially if there's someone to sprinkle salt on them.

4 – MEAT AND POULTRY

Meat on boats isn't easy. Iceboxes cool off, marine refrigerators aren't as efficient as they are on land and meat goes off very quickly. Large roasts are out. So are slow-cooked stews (unless it's winter and you've got a Dickinson), and most of the recipes we know from our pre-boat lives need more fuss and space and pans than the average galley allows. Hamburgers and sausages are very messy (splattering fat in the fry pan, flare-ups on the barbecue) and, like all ground meat products, can be enthusiastic hosts to nasties like E. coli. So most of us end up eating chicken breasts or pork loin, both of which quickly fall into the same old same old category and drive us into the arms of the nearest pizza merchant.

But there are recipes—quick, simple, non-fussy and gently sophisticated—that can move supper out of the boring into the exciting. Most of these were initially developed for inexpensive, no-fuss pre-seduction suppers to be cooked in an illegal electric fry pan in a student residence, recipes to be both cooked and consumed with a bottle of wine. Most of them can be made with frozen meat, which cuts easily and quickly with a sharp knife and is semi-thawed by the time it gets into the pan. Chicken thighs are cheaper and more flavourful than breasts, and you can quickly learn to take out the bone with a sharp knife.

african chicken stew

Serves 4, with leftovers

I once spent a lot of time on Omaha Beach, eating chicken out of a can. It was an American beach, so there was lots of it, and I finally got quite fond of its bland, tasteless innocence. Later on I found a lot of other cans to choose from, and a big sergeant from New Orleans showed me how to jazz it up.

8 chicken thighs, bone-in
1 onion, sliced thin
2 cloves garlic, chopped
1 tsp [5 mL] cayenne
1 tsp [5 mL] dried mint
½ can [12 oz/398 mL]
    diced tomatoes
½ can [6½ oz/200 mL]
    coconut milk
3 Tbsp [45 mL] peanut butter
2 bananas, peeled and sliced
salt
lemon juice

Heat a fry pan and fry chicken, skin side down, 2 minutes over medium heat. Turn chicken and cook another 2 minutes. Add onion and garlic, and cook 2 minutes, stirring well. Stir in cayenne and mint. Add tomatoes, bring to the boil then simmer 10 minutes. Add coconut milk and peanut butter, and stir well to dissolve peanut butter. Bring to the boil, add bananas and cook 10 minutes. Stir in salt to taste and sprinkle with lemon juice.

chicken and peanuts

Serves 2

This is a reputation maker that takes 20 minutes and is better than any takeout you can get delivered to the dock.

1 whole skinless boneless chicken
    breast or 4 deboned thighs
1 tsp [5 mL] cornstarch
1 tsp [5 mL] red pepper flakes
2 Tbsp [30 mL] olive oil
1 medium onion, chopped coarse
1 packet dry roasted or
    salted peanuts
2 Tbsp [30 mL] soy sauce
2 Tbsp [30 mL] whisky (or
    whatever you've got)

Cut the chicken into bite-sized pieces and toss with the cornstarch and pepper flakes. Heat the oil in a fry pan over medium heat. Add chicken and cook 1 minute. Turn the chicken and cook another minute. Add the onion and cook 2 minutes. Add the peanuts and cook 3 minutes. Add the soy sauce and whisky, and cook 1 minute. Add ¼ cup [60 mL] water, stir well and cook 3–4 minutes. Serve with rice.

chicken and rye

Serves 2

Ridiculously easy, and leftovers are very good cold for the next day's lunch. We originally made this with Jack Daniel's, one windy winter night at the Keats Island dock. You can use sherry, brandy or even Grand Marnier.

2 Tbsp [30 mL] oil
3 cloves garlic, chopped coarse
1 whole skinless boneless chicken
    breast, cut in 8 pieces
½ tsp [2 mL] salt
½ tsp [2 mL] pepper
1 heaping tsp [7 mL] tarragon,
    or ½ tsp [2 mL] thyme
2 Tbsp [30 mL] rye whisky

Heat the oil in a fry pan over medium-high heat and cook garlic 1 minute. Add the chicken and fry each side 3 minutes to colour it. Add salt, pepper, tarragon and whisky, and toss. Turn heat to medium, cover and cook 5 minutes. Add ¼ cup [60 mL] water, cover and cook 5 minutes.

chicken and grapes

Serves 2

Another ridiculously easy variation on frying up a bit of chicken in a pan. A good dish for a romantic "I knew you'd like boats as soon as you came aboard ..." evening.

**1 whole skinless boneless
    chicken breast**
1 Tbsp [15 mL] flour *or*
    Bisquick or cornstarch
salt and pepper to taste
2 Tbsp [30 mL] oil *or* **butter**
bunch seedless green grapes
½ tsp [2 mL] tarragon
½ glass white wine *or*
    cider *or* **apple juice**
juice of 1 lemon *or* **orange**
1 candle

Cut the chicken in bite-sized pieces and toss in a plastic bag with the flour, salt and pepper. Heat a fry pan over medium heat, add butter, take chicken out of bag and fry it gently for 5 minutes. Add half the grapes and the tarragon, toss well and cook 2 minutes. Add the wine, cook 5 minutes and sprinkle with lemon juice.

While the chicken is cooking, pull the rest of the grapes off the stems and let them sit in a bit of wine while you eat by candlelight. Then eat them for dessert.

chicken biryani

Serves 2

Chicken and rice can be boring. This will make a couple of chicken breasts go a long way, with less than 30 minutes' cooking.

1 whole skinless boneless chicken breast (about 350 g/12 oz)
juice of half a lemon
1/2 cup [125 mL] almonds (preferred) *or* peanuts
3 Tbsp [45 mL] oil
1 medium onion, halved and sliced thin
2 cloves garlic, chopped fine
1¼" [3 cm] piece fresh ginger, slivered
1/2 tsp [2 mL] curry powder
¼ tsp [1 mL] salt
½ tsp [2 mL] pepper
1 cup [250 mL] uncooked basmati *or* long grain rice
2 cups [500 mL] chicken stock *or* 1 chicken stock cube dissolved in 2 cups water

Cut the chicken into ½" [1 cm] cubes and marinate it in lemon juice while you get everything ready. Heat a large, dry fry pan (no oil) over medium heat. Add the almonds and stir until they colour a bit (watch carefully so they don't burn). Remove the nuts from the pan and set aside. Add 1 Tbsp [15 mL] of the oil to the pan and cook the chicken over medium-high heat until brown. Set aside. Cook the onion in the pan, stirring well, until light brown. Lower the heat, stir in the garlic and ginger, and cook 2 minutes. Stir in the curry powder, salt and pepper, and cook 30 seconds. Add the rice and stock and turn the heat to medium-high. As soon as the mixture bubbles, turn the heat down as low as it will go, cover and cook 10 minutes. Add the chicken to the rice, cover and cook 5 minutes more. Eat with yogurt and chutney.

chicken and oranges
Serves 4

2 Tbsp [30 mL] butter *or* oil
10 thin slices fresh ginger
2 skinless boneless chicken
    breasts, cut into bite-
    sized pieces
1 Tbsp [15 mL] flour *or* 1 tsp
    [5 mL] cornstarch
1 tsp [5 mL] salt
1 tsp [5 mL] pepper
2 large oranges
2 bunches green onions
chopped parsley for garnish

Heat the butter in a fry pan over medium heat, and cook ginger 2 minutes. Meanwhile, toss the chicken pieces in a bag with the flour, salt and pepper. Peel one orange, separate the segments, add to the pan and toss well. Chop the green part of the onions and set it aside. Cut the white part into 1" [2.5 cm] lengths and add to pan. Cover and cook 8 minutes over medium heat. Take out the chicken, add ½ cup [125 mL] juice from the second orange (or half a glass of sherry) and boil furiously 2 minutes. Pour the sauce over the chicken, sprinkle with parsley and chopped green onion.

25-minute chicken with tomatoes and ginger

Serves 2 hungry people

Nearly everything works well with ginger, once you get used to using it. Try this to start with.

2 Tbsp [30 mL] oil
6–8 thin slices fresh
     unpeeled ginger
1 medium onion, chopped coarse
1 lb [450 g] boneless
     chicken breasts
2 medium potatoes
2 cloves garlic, chopped fine
1 tsp [5 mL] dried thyme
     or oregano
1 tsp [5 mL] salt
1 tsp [5 mL] pepper
1 can (16 oz/500 mL)
     crushed tomatoes
squirt of tomato paste
1 glass red wine

Heat the oil in a fry pan over medium heat and fry the ginger until it smells nice. Stir in the onion and let it cook while you cut the chicken into bite-sized pieces (straight from the icebox, still frozen is fine). Add the chicken to the pan, turn up the heat and cook 5 minutes, stirring occasionally, while you cube the potatoes (don't peel them). Add the garlic, thyme, salt and pepper to the pan. Cook for 5 minutes. Add half the can of tomatoes (with their juice), the potatoes and a glass of wine. Bring to the boil and squirt in some tomato paste. Turn the heat to low, cover the pan, cook 15 minutes and there's supper. Put the unused tomatoes in the icebox, and tomorrow you will make ...

pappa al pomodoro

Serves 4

This isn't actually a meat dish, but it's here because you can make this stew-like soup that Italians call Pappa al Pomodoro *with the half-can of tomatoes left over from 25-minute chicken with tomatoes and ginger, previous page.*

1 medium onion, chopped small
1 Tbsp [15 mL] olive oil
5 thin slices of fresh
    ginger (optional)
1/2 can [16 oz/500 mL]
    crushed tomatoes
small glass wine
water
squirt of tomato paste
two slices good bread
salt

Fry onion 5 minutes in olive oil with fresh ginger. Add the tomatoes and bring to a boil. Add wine, four wine glasses of water and a good squirt of tomato paste. Bring to boil. Tear up bread and add to the pan. Cover and cook 15 minutes. Give it a good stir to break up the bread completely, add a bit more salt if you need it. You don't need stock—the bread gives it the flavour. And good bread, unsliced, keeps longer than supermarket sliced. The ginger isn't traditional, so leave it out if you like.

pork chops and apples

Serves 2

Dead easy. Just remember to take the nutmeg when you get on the boat.

1 Tbsp [15 mL] oil
2 substantial pork chops
1 medium onion, sliced thick
1 clove garlic, chopped
1 further Tbsp [15 mL] oil
2 Granny Smith crisp green
    apples, cored, seeded
    and cut into eighths
salt and pepper
½ cup [125 mL] white wine
    or apple juice
½ tsp [2 mL] grated nutmeg

Heat a fry pan over medium heat, add 1 Tbsp oil and fry chops 3 minutes on each side. Add onion and garlic, and cook 2 minutes. Push the chops and onion to the sides of the pan. Add the further 1 Tbsp oil and the apples. Sprinkle with salt and pepper to taste, and toss together well. Add the wine, cover and cook 10 minutes. Sprinkle on the nutmeg and eat.

spicy peanut pork chops (or chicken breast)

Serves 2

You can cook this dish with 2 chicken breast halves instead of the pork chops.

1 Tbsp [15 mL] oil
4 thin slices fresh ginger
½ tsp [2 mL] red pepper flakes
    or 4 little hot peppers
2 pork chops
½ cup [125 mL] Super All-Purpose
    Peanut Sauce (p. 28)
3 Tbsp [45 mL] water
    or beer *or* cola

Heat a fry pan over medium heat, add oil and fry ginger and pepper 2 minutes. Push them to the sides of the pan and add chops so they are in direct contact with the pan. Cook 5 minutes, turn and cook 5 minutes more over medium heat. Spoon on the peanut sauce and water, cover and cook 5 minutes more over low heat. That's it!

corned beef hash

Serves 1

An essential for anybody who cooks on boats, or who camps, or who suddenly decides to be a bachelor. Breakfast, lunch or supper, it's a big, filling dish that nourishes your soul. I learned it first in France, cooked in a tin mess kit. You need a grater for the potatoes, and I guarantee you'll use it a lot.

1 can corned beef
1 egg
2 large potatoes, unpeeled, grated
salt and pepper to taste
1 medium onion, chopped fine
1 tsp [5 mL] thyme *or* rosemary
2 Tbsp [30 mL] oil
1 tsp [5 mL] dry mustard
1 Tbsp [15 mL] oil

Chop up the corned beef and mix it in a bowl with the egg, potato, salt, pepper, onion and thyme. Use your hands and really squish everything together. Heat a fry pan over medium-high heat, add the 2 Tbsp oil, then put in the corned beef mixture and pat it down with a fork to make a dense cake. Sprinkle the mustard over top, turn the heat to medium, cover and cook about 10 minutes or until the bottom is brown. Put a plate over the top of the pan, flip it over and slide the cake back into the pan along with 1 Tbsp oil. Cook uncovered for another 5–10 minutes until brown underneath. Slide out and eat immediately.

ginger

Gravol works if you take it two hours before you need it. But seasickness is a denial disease that nobody will admit to until it happens, by which time it's too late to imagine that anything you swallow will remain with you long enough to have any effect. Dying is the only immediate and surefire remedy, but it's not very popular on small boats. There are wristbands and patches and even meditative procedures—one gale-warning March night we had a man who sat cross-legged on deck just forward of the mast all the way from Nanaimo to the bell buoy. He wasn't sick but he was a considerable nuisance.

The easiest and best thing I've ever found for seasickness is fresh ginger. All supermarkets and most corner stores sell it, a light brown and slightly knobbly root. The Chinese have used it for thousands of years as an anti-nausea folk remedy. Seasickness, morning sickness, car sickness, even hangovers—they all retreat from root ginger, and there are very few stomach upsets that don't respond favourably.

I first discovered ginger tea in Malaysia, where it is drunk very strong and very spicy in small cups after big dinners. Back in Canada it quickly became a necessary staple for just about any trip. We make it strong and carry it in a pop bottle, ready to be diluted and taken hot or cold, with whisky or without it. Kids like it cut with soda water. Whatever way you take it, it works wonders, a great drink winter or summer.

Ginger is probably the most used and least mentioned ingredient in good Chinese food. Vegetable stir-fries, pork dishes, chicken dishes, soups and dim sum—all have a little ginger somewhere, sliced or grated. Because of its versatility, ginger is particularly useful on boats. Use it to jazz up a couple of pork chops, brighten a can of soup, add to a few blackberries you might find in fall. I put it in beets, carrots or fried rice, and in spicy noodles and chicken soup. I use it to invigorate a jar of store-bought tomato sauce and I even grate it over ice cream. Just a few slices do wonders for a pan of fried chicken.

Buy ginger carefully—it should have nice shiny skin, not shrivelled—and keep it in the icebox in a zip-lock bag. Sometimes at home I fill a jar with chunks of ginger, then fill the jar with sherry. Fish out a chunk to chop up and add to what you're cooking (the sherry gives it an extra punch), or pour yourself a slug from the jar to sip while getting supper (in case you get seasick at anchor). If you're tired and headachey after a day in the sun, cut two thin slices of the cold root and get your mate to lightly massage your temples with the slices on the tips of his middle fingers. And if you're not tired and bitchy, do it anyway—like most popular Chinese remedies, it boots up the libido.

ginger tea
Makes 4–5 qts [4–5 L]

6"–8" [15–20 cm] piece fresh
  unpeeled ginger, sliced thin
4 or 5 quarts [4–5 L] of water
½ cup [125 mL] brown
  sugar *or* honey
1 whole lemon

Combine all but the lemon in a large pot and bring to the boil. Add the lemon (uncut, unpeeled) and simmer 30 minutes. Strain into a jug with the juice of the lemon (boiling makes it a lot juicier so you won't need a juicer). Cool it and keep it in the fridge until you need it, or freeze it solid in a plastic bottle and use it as a coolant in the icebox on the boat, drinking what melts.

5 – FRESH SEAFOOD

My first real boat was an ancient amateur re-rigged 2½-ton Hilyard, a gaff-rigged sloop, without winches and before nylon, which meant that trimming sail or even just going about was a complicated, back-straining, palm-stripping process. It involved a sophisticated method of jiggling wooden blocks and an even more sophisticated method of steering, known as "bumlock." You can figure that one out for yourself—single-handed, helm hard over because she went across the wind slower than a haltered cow, and since I needed both hands to trim and cleat the mainsheet, the only way to steer and get back up into the wind was to grab the tiller with the seat of my pants.

In those days the Solent (on the south coast of England) was a good place to fish for mackerel, which, like tuna, are attracted to just about anything bright and shiny that flutters in the water like a wounded fish. I learned this the hard way. A hand-held rod will always catch more fish than one in a mounted rod holder because there's more movement to it. Anybody holding a rod naturally wriggles about, grabs a beer, reads the chart, takes a deep breath, and all these small movements are transmitted to the lure in the water. I always dragged a line over the stern and twitched it occasionally without much luck, but I could be just about a hundred percent sure of hooking a fish at the moment of most activity, right at the crucial moment of going about, both hands (and buttocks) busy, the boat dickering in stays and the little bell on the line saying fish fish fish.

And by the time we were about, settled down on the new tack, a bigger fish had eaten the back half of my mackerel and left me with the head. The same thing happened to me a couple of years ago off Cape Mudge, where the rockfish we caught close to the kelp beds were grabbed by opportunistic lingcod. The moral of this story is if you've got fish, do something about it immediately. That is also the best counsel anybody can give you when it comes to cooking fish. The quicker you can get it into the pan, the better it's going to taste, and the less you do to it, the better. We used to haul in the mackerel, gut it, crank up the Primus right there in the cockpit, and cook it in a dry fry pan liberally dusted with coarse salt. Which brings us to ...

shio yaki
Serves 2

This is the simplest way I know of cooking fish for two people. It was given to me on a fishboat in northern Japan, where the climate, vegetation, marine life and fishing methods are almost exactly the same as on the north end of Vancouver Island. The recipe works for cod, snapper or any other white fish, and it's particularly good with pink salmon or chum—almost anything so long as it's very fresh. But it must be fresh, fresh and fresh.

Sprinkle both sides of a piece of fish 1" [2.5 cm] thick with 1 tsp [5 mL] of salt, and leave it for 30 minutes (shower, polish brass, watch sunset, wash underwear, a quickie—your choice). Heat a dry fry pan—no oil—on medium-high heat (if you flick drops of water on the pan they sizzle), and lay fish in. Don't move it, and no peeking underneath. Cook 3 minutes, turn it over and cook 4 minutes. Let it sit 2 minutes and eat. The Japanese, of course, eat it with rice.

If there are more of you, you're better off with a fish stew. And you might want to give it a fancy name. Such as:

matelote de fevrier, or my aunt sallie's cheapo 20-minute bouillabaisse

Serves 6

2 Tbsp [30 mL] butter
1 medium onion, chopped coarse
2 cloves garlic, chopped fine
1 lb [450 g] mushrooms, halved
2 Tbsp [30 mL] canned anchovies
    or Asian fish sauce
½ can (14 oz/398 mL) crushed
    tomatoes *or* two chopped
    ripe tomatoes
1 cup [250 mL] apple juice,
    or white wine *or* beer
1 tsp [5 mL] crushed thyme
2 lbs [1 g] white fish cut into
    1½" (4 cm) pieces
1 oz [30 mL] rye whisky
½ cup [125 mL] plain yogurt
    or sour cream
2 Tbsp [30 mL] soy sauce

Heat the butter in a fry pan over low heat. Add the onion and garlic, cover and cook 5 minutes. Stir in the mushrooms and anchovies, add the tomatoes, apple juice and thyme, and simmer 10 minutes, uncovered. Add the fish, pushing the pieces into the sauce. Bring to the boil over high heat, then lower heat, cover and simmer 6 minutes. Stir in the whisky, cook 1 minute, stir in the yogurt and soy sauce and heat briefly. Eat with bread and gusto.

fish with peanut butter sauce

Serves 2 (or more, if you have more fish)

3 Tbsp [45 mL] Super All-Purpose
    Peanut Sauce (p. 28),
    made with orange juice
    rather than beer
1 tsp [5 mL] soy sauce
1 lb [450 g] fresh fish (snapper,
    salmon, cod, etc.)

Mix peanut sauce and soy sauce. Spread over the fish and steam in a covered pot for 10 minutes. Or fry the fish and spread it with the sauce after cooking.

fresh crab

If it's fresh, all you have to do is cook it right. Forget all the nonsense about a humongous pot of boiling water (which will use all your propane and fill the cabin with steam), and just dump a bottle of beer (or cider) into a pot big enough to hold the crab with the lid on. Add 2 strips of orange zest, a bay leaf and a whole clove of garlic, put the crab in (upside down), cover, bring to the boil, reduce heat and cook an absolute maximum of 12 minutes. Plunge the crab into a bucket of seawater for a couple of minutes and eat immediately. Or you can leave it in the cooling water another 15 minutes and keep the crab (in its shell, in the icebox) for lunch next day.

Two things to remember:
1. Learn to pick up the crab safely. Go at it from behind, put three fingers firmly on top of the shell and slide your thumb under the belly. Press hard with all fingers and thumb. While the crab may wave its legs furiously, the pincers can't reach you—if you hold on tight.
2. Everything inside the shell is edible, except the grey fingers snugged up to the body. Throw those away. Lining the shell is a thickish layer of orange-yellow fat, and in the shell are a couple of spoonfuls of liquid. Both of these are enormously flavourful, so scrape off the fat and put it in a cup with the liquid. Add a pinch of Tabasco sauce and a squeeze of lemon juice (or a spoonful of rye whisky), then stir them both into ½ cup [125 mL] mayonnaise. Use this mix as a dipping sauce for the crab, or as a sauce over pasta.

plain or fancy clams or mussels
Serves 2 gluttons

1 Tbsp [15 mL] olive oil
1 medium onion, chopped fine
1 clove garlic, chopped fine
10 thin slices fresh ginger
1 cup [250 mL] beer, *or* cider, white
    wine, chicken stock *or* water
2 lbs [1 kg] fresh clams *or* mussels
juice of 1 lemon

Heat the oil over medium heat in a pot big enough to hold the clams with the lid on. Fry the onion, garlic and ginger 3 minutes. Add the beer, bring to the boil, add clams, or mussels, and cook covered over high heat 3 minutes. Uncover the pot, and if all shells are open, sprinkle with lemon juice and eat immediately, with bread to sop up the juices. If the shells aren't open, cook another minute. Just don't overcook.

If you want to be fancy, pour off the cooking juices into mugs, add an ounce [30 mL] of vodka or Scotch to each, sprinkle with cayenne pepper and slurp down while it's still hot.

pink salmon aboard (and three things about tying up)

There is much to be said for tying up alongside a docked fishboat. You have to have lots of fenders ready, and of course you have to ask permission. The asking may include the offering of a drink, discreet inquiries about how things are going and a certain amount of sympathy, and of course you must establish at what ungodly hour they will be leaving in the morning. If all is conducted in diplomatic terms, the talk may well conclude with the offer of a fish for your supper. It won't be a sockeye or a spring, but probably a pink. A fresh pink, kept cold, and fried or barbecued in steaks or fillets (certainly not baked whole) is a very good fish indeed, and one we should be learning a lot more about. Fillet it or cut it crosswise into steaks as soon as you get it, and cook it all. What you don't eat for supper will keep until tomorrow and make a salad or fishcakes or sandwiches.

Shio Yaki (p. 56) is an excellent way to cook pink salmon, but if you don't have 30 minutes to salt it and you want to eat immediately, just fry it. Fillets with the skin on need nothing more than a dry pan. Heat the pan over medium-high heat, lay in the fillets skin side down, sprinkle lightly with salt, cover and cook 5 minutes. Now comes the gourmet bit that turns your modest piece of salmon into something special. But it involves thinking. You have to choose. Orange juice, apple juice, white wine, red wine, cider, vermouth, gin—you must have one of them onboard, so choose one and pour ½ cup [125 mL] of it over the fish, put the lid back on and cook 2 more minutes. The fish juices and whatever you added will make a pan sauce. Gin makes a particularly nice pan sauce. Measure out about 1 Tbsp [15 mL] of it, because pouring it out of the bottle is dangerous over a hot stove. I've even used Scotch and rum, which both make nice sauces.

Cook the rest of the fish—just pan-fry it, no sauce, and it will keep well until the next day for salads, sandwiches or fishcakes.

Three things to remember about tying up to fishboats: 1) make sure the bitter ends of your lines are secured on your boat, not theirs, for easier and quicker casting off; 2) don't get over-enthusiastic and try to outdrink a fisherman—it may seem a good idea at the time but not the morning after; 3) if they mention the government (code words are "bloody fisheries" or "them bastards in Ottawa"), nod, look sympathetic and keep your mouth shut.

beach oysters

On a low tide and a rocky beach almost anywhere north of Lasqueti, you should find beach oysters. They're not the little ones you slurp raw in fancy restaurants, they're big and they need to be cooked.

The simplest way is put them on the barbecue, flat side of the shell up, and cook until the shell opens. Sprinkle with Tabasco sauce, or lemon juice or mayonnaise or sesame oil or Scotch, and eat either with a knife and fork or stuffed between two slices of bread. Messy but nice.

Or you can fry them. Opening beach oysters on-board can be very bad for decks, so be careful. I suggest you put them on the barbecue until the shells open just a little bit, when you can pop in a kitchen knife and sever the muscle. Fry them in butter over medium heat, sprinkle with pepper and lemon juice, or soy sauce or teriyaki sauce or Tabasco sauce or Worcestershire sauce, and eat.

fancy oyster stew

Serves 4

An oyster stew made of beach oysters is a wondrous thing on a cold winter's day. It sounds a bit complicated, but it's dead easy. You've read the tide tables, you know where you're going to find the oysters (this is a winter trip, an occasion well worth advance planning) and you have bought a couple of extra ingredients, like a small carton of cream, some fresh dill and a decent loaf of bread. I've also taken (at various times) gin, champagne, Jack Daniel's and Captain Morgan's rum, and one Christmas in Heriot Bay, when the guests missed their plane and didn't arrive with the cooked turkey they'd promised, we ate this stew, with a bottle of Scotch, for Christmas dinner.

4 or 5 big beach oysters (or a 1 lb/500 mL tub if you don't want to take the boat out)
2 Tbsp [30 mL] butter
1 large onion, chopped
1 stalk celery, chopped fine
1 clove garlic, chopped fine
1 large potato, diced ½" [1 cm]
1 sweet red pepper, diced
½ tsp [2 mL] salt
½ tsp [2 mL] pepper
1 tsp [5 mL] paprika
½ cup [125 mL] white wine *or* water *or* canned clam juice

1 cup [250 mL] milk
1 tsp [5 mL] Worcestershire sauce *or* Asian fish sauce
½ cup [125 mL] half-and-half cream (or, if you're desperate, evaporated milk)
juice of 1 lemon

Open the oysters while you heat the butter in a pot over medium heat. Fry the onion, celery and garlic 5 minutes. Add the potato, red pepper, salt, pepper, paprika and wine. Cover and cook 10 minutes. Cut the oysters into 3 or 4 pieces and add them to the pan with their juices. Cook 4 minutes. Add milk and Worcestershire sauce, heat through almost to the boil, lower heat and stir in cream for no more than 30 seconds (boiling will make it curdle), and remove from heat immediately. Sprinkle with lemon juice and eat.

Once you've made a good oyster stew, you'll want to do it again.

6 – SALMON ON THE SHELF

Some of us catch fish. Most of us don't. Most of us give up. Others buy one and lie. Some open cans. I've given up on trolling for salmon. I seem to get lucky jigging for cod at anchor and even luckier with one of those folding crab traps that you toss in with 20-lb test on a good stiff rod, but I don't think any boat should be without a can or two of salmon in the galley. Canned salmon is enormously versatile as an ingredient, hot or cold, and if you're really desperate you can just open it and eat it straight out of the can, heated or not. Sockeye is best—it costs more but it has a lot more flavour, colour and body than pink.

salmon sandwiches

Spread mayonnaise on 2 slices of bread, then add thin-sliced onion or cucumber or a couple of lettuce leaves or even thin-sliced cabbage—a good salmon sandwich needs something with a bit of crunch to it. Put the salmon on last and eat the sandwich at once, before things get soggy. Tomatoes are best alongside rather than actually in the sandwich.

salmon potato salad
Serves 4

1 can [7½ oz/213 g]
    sockeye salmon
3 medium potatoes
1 medium onion, chopped fine
1 clove garlic, chopped fine
1 head lettuce *or* ½ small
    green cabbage
salt and pepper
3 Tbsp [45 mL] olive oil
1 Tbsp [15 mL] lemon
    juice *or* vinegar

Open the salmon and break it up with a fork. Put potatoes in a pot, cover with water and boil. While they're cooking, chop the onion and garlic fine. Tear the lettuce into bite-sized pieces (or shred the cabbage). Dice the potatoes while still hot, put them in a bowl, salt and pepper generously and pour the olive oil over them. Add the onion, garlic and greens and toss well. Sprinkle with lemon juice, toss again and then add the salmon. Eat while it's still warm. Whatever you make or cook with canned salmon, it should always be the last thing you add.

salmon chowder

Serves 4

Chowder doesn't have to be clam chowder.

3 Tbsp [45 mL] olive oil
3 medium potatoes, diced
    (don't peel them)
1 medium onion, chopped fine
2 cloves of garlic, chopped fine
1 can [14 oz/398 mL]
    crushed tomatoes
V tsp [2 mL] rosemary *or* thyme
¾ cup [175 mL] wine *or* canned
    clam juice *or* 1 chicken
    stock cube dissolved in 1
    cup [250 mL] hot water
1 can [7½ oz/213 g] salmon
chopped parsley for garnish

Heat the olive oil in a pot over medium heat and fry the potatoes 3 minutes. Add the onion and garlic, and cook 3 minutes. Stir in the tomatoes and rosemary, and cook 5 minutes. Add the wine, cover and simmer 3 minutes. Finally, add the salmon. Stir to spread it through the chowder, taste for salt and pepper, and cook 20 minutes max. Top with chopped parsley if you've got it.

Curry powder makes the chowder different. Chopped fresh tomatoes are good in season, and a little sherry is a fine thing to add immediately before you serve it.

sesame salmon stir-fry

Serves 4

Salmon and rice is a good, quick one-pot dinner, a kind of Korean stir-fry.

1 cup [250 mL] rice
2 cups [500 mL] water
2 Tbsp [30 mL] olive oil
1 medium onion, chopped fine
2 cloves garlic, chopped fine
½ head of lettuce *or* cabbage
    or any greens, chopped
    as fine as possible
½ tsp [2 mL] cayenne pepper
    or red pepper flakes
1 tsp [5 mL] sesame oil
1 can [7½ oz/213 g] salmon
1 tsp [5 mL] whatever dried
    herb you have

Combine the rice and water in a pot, bring to the boil, then cover and cook 15 minutes over low heat. Tip cooked rice out on to a plate. Wash out the pan, heat the oil on high heat and stir-fry the onion, garlic, lettuce and cayenne for 2 minutes. Sprinkle with sesame oil, add the rice, mix together well and cook 2 minutes over medium heat. Add the salmon and herbs and toss lightly.

Don't keep sesame oil on the boat all winter, it goes rancid. But a case of canned salmon will last you for a single-handed circumnavigation.

fishcakes

Serves 2

Canned salmon, canned tuna or leftover fish or crab—all make fishcakes. Purists make their fishcakes with fish and potatoes; others substitute cooked rice for the potatoes. There are three secrets to making fishcakes: first, use the right proportions of potato (or rice) and fish; second, eat them as they come out of the pan; third (very important), make sure the cook gets a proper share.

2 cups [500 mL] cold mashed
    potatoes
1 cup [250 mL] canned salmon,
    tuna, cod, whatever,
    or cold cooked fish
1 medium onion, chopped fine
1 egg
handful of chopped parsley
½ tsp [2 mL] pepper
bread crumbs *or* flour
2 Tbsp [30 mL] oil for frying

Mix all the ingredients (except bread crumbs) together vigorously and roll into balls as large as eggs. Flatten each ball into a round as thick as your finger. Pat bread crumbs into each side and fry the cakes over medium heat for a few minutes, until crisp and brown. Eat with ketchup, Worcestershire sauce, salsa or a slice of crisp fried bacon.

7 – BARBECUE

Dried applewood and mesquite charcoal are undoubtedly the best fuel there is for barbecues, but not on boats. Apart from storage problems (very few boats have woodsheds) there are the ashes to contend with, and the sparks and the smoke. Charcoal briquettes have fewer storage problems, but a bag of briquettes stored in the lazaret or in the bilge is quite capable of spontaneous combustion—particularly if they're the self-igniting ones. Propane is the answer—maybe not quite so hot, but safer and cleaner. A boat just isn't a backyard.

And that's the first thing to remember for successful boat barbecues. Fat and flames and flare-ups are hard to cope with, so you learn to avoid them. No hamburgers or lamb chops, pork chops only if they've been well trimmed of the fat around the edge, no oily marinades, no skin on the chicken before cooking, no sausages except maybe nice lean weisswurst. If you're just a little selective about what you cook, you'll be a lot happier about the cleanup. And if you can learn not to overcrowd your little barbecue (dinner for six just isn't on), you'll be a lot happier with the results.

grilled garlic bread

This is the time to buy yourself a teflon basting brush, anywhere from $5 to $25 in a kitchen store. Unlike a bristle brush, it can stand heat up to 400°F [200°C] and stays completely free of any rancid fat odours. Grill thick slices of bread until lightly toasted, rub each side vigorously with a split clove of garlic, then brush lightly with olive oil and grill a few seconds longer. This way you'll get no flare-ups. Good bread is better than supermarket sliced.

barbecued flank steak

Serves 4 (or 2 teenagers)

If you like steak, try this. No marinade, no matter what Martha says. A flank steak has no waste and no bones, so it's enough for dinner and there will be leftovers for beef salad tomorrow.

1 flank steak, 1½ lbs [675 g]
salt and pepper
no oil no oil no oil

Heat the barbecue for 15 minutes to get it really hot. Sprinkle the steak with salt and pepper, throw it on the centre of the barbecue, close the lid and grill it for 4 minutes *exactly*. Flip it over, put the lid down again quickly and cook for 3 minutes *exactly*. (Cooking it any longer will make it tough.) Take it off the grill and let it sit for 5 minutes. Slice it very thin across the grain, and serve immediately.

bbq pork chops for two

Serves 2

One thick pork chop cut in two after cooking tastes better than two thin pork chops grilled separately. And pork with the bone in tastes better than boneless. But whatever you do, trim off the fat with a sharp knife before barbecuing, and no marinades. You can brine the chops for an hour—this will not only make the chop more tender, it will also intensify the essential flavour of the meat itself. I use seawater as a brine (but not at dock or in a crowded anchorage). If you want to cut a green apple crosswise into thick slices (don't bother peeling or coring it) and grill them alongside the pork, that's nice too.

1 thick bone-in pork chop
pepper

Put the chop in a bowl of seawater for 30–60 minutes before cooking. Drain, pat dry, sprinkle well with pepper and pat the pepper in. Heat the barbecue for 10 minutes. Grill the chop at the highest heat for 5 minutes, turn the chop over and grill another 5 minutes. Thin chops take less time, but can get tough very easily.

chicken on the grill

Take the skin off the chicken before barbecuing. Boneless is fine. Wings, no. I brine and cook chicken as I do pork chops (see above), but cook them 5 minutes longer, or I cook them in foil packets with or without the skin (see p. 77).

cedar-barbecued salmon

You can't cook a whole salmon on any barbecue, let alone a boat barbecue. You can overcook it, burn it, undercook it, have it fall apart, but you can't cook it properly. The best way to cook salmon is on a cedar plank. Make sure it's untreated cedar. You can buy offcuts of 1" [2.5 cm] cedar plank at any lumberyard, or find bits of it on the beach. Soak the plank in water for a couple of hours—hang it over the side with a fishing weight attached to keep it submerged. Heat the grill for 15 minutes, lay a salmon fillet or steak on the plank, sprinkle with salt, cover the barbecue and cook the salmon over high heat 10–15 minutes. Check for doneness, take it off the fire, sprinkle well with the juice of half an orange, and serve.

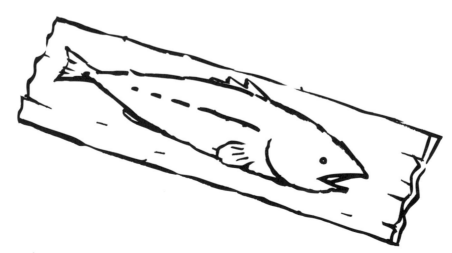

grilled vegetables

Sweet peppers

Halve peppers, remove seeds and cut flesh into 1" [2 cm] strips. Cook skin side down 10 minutes over a hot fire. Immediately put the peppers in a plastic bag and twist to expel air. Leave them for 10–30 minutes, take them out and most of the skin will rub off. Don't wash them—it dilutes the taste, and a few flecks of burnt skin won't hurt you. Drizzle with olive oil and eat hot or cold.

Asparagus

Snap butt ends off the spears, oil them very lightly and grill 3–4 minutes over a hot fire. Roll over, grill another 3 minutes, take off fire, sprinkle with salt.

Green Beans

Cook the same way as asparagus, but for a bit less time.

Lettuce

This may sound peculiar, but grilled radicchio is a famous dish in Italy. However, radicchio is hard to find in most marinas. Romaine has much the same structure as radicchio, so buy a head, cut it lengthwise into quarters, brush very lightly with olive oil and grill over high heat until the edges char a bit. Take off the fire, sprinkle with salt and a bit more oil, and eat immediately.

Carrots
Cut lengthwise into quarters and cook the same way as asparagus.

Potatoes
Cut into ½" [1 cm] chunks. Put them on a double sheet of aluminum foil and roll them around in a little oil, salt and pepper. Fold over the edges of the foil to seal, and put the package on the barbecue, while it's heating up, for 15 minutes. Leave it there while you cook the meat, and the potatoes should be done. Cooking times vary—if they're not ready, give them another 5 minutes.

Green Peas
Enclose whole shelled peas in foil, as for potatoes, but with a little butter. Cook for 10 minutes, sprinkle with salt and eat immediately.

Corn on the Cob
Soak the corn in a bucket of seawater for 30 minutes. Forget all the nonsense about peeling back the husks and taking off the silk, just put them in the bucket as they come. Grill them over a hot fire with the lid down for 10 minutes, turning occasionally. The husks will char and give a lovely smoky flavour to the corn. Take off one ear and strip back the husk a little bit to check for doneness. Eat as soon as the corn is done. The silk will come off with the husk. Butter is messy in a cockpit, so try sprinkling the cob with salt and then squeezing a fresh lime over it the way they do in Oaxaca.

foil-packet dinners

... are not as complicated as they are made out to be. You need two sheets of foil, one laid diagonally across the other (eight corners sticking out, right?). Don't make big packets—single servings are best. Lay whatever you want to cook diagonally across the top sheet and season with Basic Quick Peanut Sauce (p. 29), butter, salt and pepper, sesame oil, sliced apples, chopped onion, garlic, whatever whatever whatever. Add 2 Tbsp [30 mL] liquid (orange juice, apple juice, whisky, sake, beer, wine or what-have-you), fold over the top sheet and roll the corners together. Then do the same with the bottom sheet. Put the packets on a very hot grill, put the lid down and cook 15 minutes, which should be long enough for chicken breast or salmon or a bit of cod or a dozen clams.

   Foil packets are the finger painting of cooking, and they always taste wonderful. You can warm up leftover rice, cold chickpeas or even pasta this way—just add a very little oil to the packet. Cook pork chops with marmalade, let asparagus spears cook in butter and their own juices, or combine chicken with cherry tomatoes—there's no limit to what you can do with a roll of aluminum foil and a sense of adventure. If your barbecue doesn't have a lid, then drape a bit more foil over the packets to speed up the cooking time.

cabbage

The secret to cooking on boats is knowing that the rules are different. You're not entertaining, you're not at home with unlimited supplies, a dishwasher and a collection of cookbooks. But you've usually got a crew with an appetite as impatient as it's hungry, and if you can regularly have supper in front of them less than 30 minutes after the anchor goes down, you'll be top of the list for gold in the Best Person On Boat Olympics.

Forget Emeril, Martha, even Julia. Forget the gourmet magazines, your grandma's secret spaghetti sauce recipe and the class you once took on making *foie gras* an essential part of your life, and remind yourself that a galley is no place for flambés or consommés. You're not a chef, you're a cook. I've cooked strapped in on sailboats, commercial fishboats, working tugboats and, for two years, a Lightning with a Primus and a leaky cockpit awning. They're all the same: not enough room or pots or spices, and always something missing.

But with your good, big serves-four fry pan with a tight-fitting lid, and your 4–5 qt/L saucepan that fits the same lid as the fry pan, and some salt and pepper, mustard powder, cooking oil, booze (sherry, rye, Scotch, red wine or beer) and one dried herb (rosemary, thyme or oregano), there are very few recipes that you can't adapt to a quick sea-going version. If you also have a can of diced tomatoes, another of white beans, a can of tuna, a tube of tomato paste and some chicken stock cubes, you're set to become a legend.

The one thing you can't do without is flexibility. Take something really humble, like a cabbage.

cabbage 101

A head of lettuce will go limp overnight, but a good, big, shiny green cabbage will keep, unrefrigerated, for the better part of a week uncut, and three or four days cut, if wrapped tight in a plastic bag. Cut the cabbage into big wedges, then grate them on the coarse side of the grater, grate some carrot to go with it, and toss it with a quick dressing of peanut butter, salt, pepper, a pinch of sugar and whatever you have on board to drink (apple juice, beer, sherry, white wine, orange juice—they all work with cabbage). You can dress it up with thin-sliced apple or a few of your cocktail-hour peanuts (or walnuts or almonds, whatever you've got) or toss in a can of sockeye or tuna if you want a quick summer lunch. Shredded cabbage is foolproof and indestructible.

cabbage 201

Serves 2

The same cabbage as in 101, but quick-cooked. The one important thing about quick-cooked cabbage is "quick"—a maximum of 5 minutes.

1 green cabbage
2 Tbsp [30 mL] cooking oil
fresh unpeeled ginger
salt and pepper
soy sauce
3–4 Tbsp [45–60 mL] beer (or whatever you're drinking)

Slice the cabbage ½" [1 cm] thick, removing the core as you go, so you get long, thin strips. Heat the oil in a fry pan over medium heat. Grate ginger directly into the pan and fry for a minute, then add the sliced cabbage, salt and pepper to taste, and stir-fry about 3 minutes. Sprinkle with soy sauce, add the beer, toss well, cover and cook another minute. Turn off the heat and let it sit for a minute, covered, and you've got instant Chinese food.

Cabbage 201 is very versatile—you can add thin-sliced ham for the last minute of cooking (I've even used cubed Spam in desperation), canned fish, thin-sliced mushrooms, halved cherry tomatoes or a combination.

cabbage 301

Serves 2 with leftovers

You can start this slow-cooked winter dish 45 minutes from dropping the anchor. Slow-cooked cabbage is totally different from quick-cooked—sweeter, richer, different in texture. And that's about as simple as I can get.

1 green cabbage
1 medium onion
2 Tbsp [30 mL] cooking oil
1 tsp [5 mL] salt
pepper
1 garlic sausage, sliced ½" [1 cm]
    thick (smoked meat keeps
    better on boats than fresh)
half a bottle of beer

Quarter the cabbage, cut out the stalk and slice it ¾" [2 cm] thick. Quarter the onion and slice it thin. Heat the oil in a deep pan over medium heat, add the onion and fry 1 minute. Add the cabbage, salt and a lot of black pepper, and turn over to coat everything with oil. Cook 3 minutes. Add the garlic sausage and beer. If you've got room in the pot, add peeled potatoes in walnut-sized chunks at the same time as the garlic sausage. Bring to the boil, cover and simmer over the lowest heat for 45 minutes, stirring occasionally and adding more beer if it starts to look dry. Eat the cabbage with good bread.

spicy cabbage

Serves 4

This is a spicy quickie that goes well with anything barbecued. Very good when you make it, and very good cold next day.

2 lbs [1 kg] cabbage, *or* sui choy
12–18 dried red peppers
    (the little hot ones)
2 Tbsp [30 mL] peanut
    oil *or* olive oil
2 Tbsp [30 mL] peanut butter
1 Tbsp [15 mL] soy sauce
2 Tbsp [30 mL] sugar

Cut cabbage into 2" [5 cm] slices. Wipe peppers and dry them. Heat peanut oil in a fry pan over high heat. Add peppers and fry 1 minute, until they are turning dark. Add cabbage and stir-fry 3 minutes over high heat. Mix peanut butter with soy sauce and sugar and add to pan. Stir well and cook 2 more minutes.

8 – PASTA AND NOODLES

Pasta is probably the most flexible ingredient you can have in a small kitchen. And certainly the easiest, either to cook well or to screw up. There are all kinds of folkloric and ridiculous systems and notions about how to tell when it's cooked properly, all the way from tossing a spoonful at the ceiling (if it sticks, it's done) to twirling it around a silver spoon (if it falls off, it isn't done). Most of them, including those two, are rubbish. The secret to good pasta is taking care, paying attention and concentrating, all of which are habits that come naturally to anybody who successfully runs a boat. You can't walk away from a pot of pasta—the skinny ones take only 4 minutes, and the big, thick, chunky ones can take 14. (That's for dried—fresh pasta cooks in even less time.) The trick is to get it out of the water some 30 seconds before it's fully cooked, and let it finish cooking in the sauce. The only way to do this is to nibble, test it between your teeth until it's only slightly chewy, then drain it immediately or get it out of the water.

If you don't really care and just want supper in a hurry, your best bet is packaged udon (Japanese or Korean noodles), which just about every corner store sells. Dumped in boiling water, they cook in 2 minutes. Stirred into a meat or vegetable stir-fry, they take about 4 minutes.

But there's a certain inexplicable joy in cooking real pasta, to say nothing of the big difference in flavour and texture when you eat it. You need a big pot of fast-boiling salted water, whatever you're going to use for a sauce ready to go, the anchor set, the wine poured, the orchestra properly rehearsed, the lamps lit and both of you ready to eat.

pasta and olive oil

Olive oil is the simplest and best-loved of pasta sauces in Italy. All it needs is good olive oil, and if you have some extraordinary, hideously expensive, estate-bottled, rich-coloured oil, then this is the time to use it. But boats are not suitable for long-term storage of good oil, so take it home with your laundry. And to really appreciate this simple a dish, you also need good pasta—something Italian, something not too heavy, something that will make a good foundation for you to taste the basic goodness of the oil.

The recipe couldn't be simpler. Into as much fast-boiling, lightly salted water as your biggest pot will hold, drop pasta for 2–4 people and cook it al dente (just the slightest bit chewy). Drain it, pepper it well and pour olive oil over top. Some like a lot of oil, some like a little, some like more salt than others. Some like Parmesan grated fresh over top, some like to add thin-sliced fresh garlic or bits of those little preserved Italian things that come in jars, like sun-dried tomatoes or baby artichokes or pickled mushrooms. You can sprinkle on red pepper flakes and/or parsley. Some like to add very thin-sliced raw button mushrooms, chopped olives or capers; some like mint, some like feta and some like canned clams (strain off the juice, save it and drink it with vodka). Whatever you choose, it's not going to take you more than 15 minutes to get supper on the table. I like hot red peppers and lots of chopped parsley—but it's your boat.

don't ask, don't tell quick pasta

Serves 2

Spaghetti doesn't need meatballs. One of my favourites is spaghetti and bread crumbs, a Sicilian 15-minute quickie that uses stale bread, garlic, hot red pepper, olive oil and anchovies. Don't be scared of the anchovies—they melt into the sauce and nobody knows they're there, but everybody says what a great sauce it is. Don't ask, don't tell.

2 slices stale good bread *or* ½ cup [125 mL] packaged bread crumbs

spaghetti—enough for 2

1 tsp [5 mL] olive oil

½ tsp [2 mL] salt

3 Tbsp [45 mL] olive oil

½ tsp [2 mL] red pepper flakes

1–3 cloves garlic, crushed

3 anchovy fillets

juice of half an orange *or* half a glass of red wine

Put the bread crumbs in a plastic bag and roll with a wine bottle until they become fine crumbs. Bring a pot of water to the boil. Add the spaghetti, 1 tsp oil and salt. It will be ready in about 7 minutes, which gives you time to make the sauce. Heat a fry pan over medium-high heat, add the 3 Tbsp olive oil and red pepper flakes, and cook 1 minute. Add the bread crumbs, cook (stirring energetically) 2 minutes. Add the garlic and anchovies and cook another 2 minutes, mashing with a fork and stirring, until the anchovies melt. Add the juice, turn up the heat and cook 2 minutes, and that's it. Put the spaghetti on plates, the sauce on the spaghetti and a drizzle of olive oil over everything, When blood oranges are in season in Sicily, they squeeze a little juice over top, or a handful of chopped parsley.

pasta fagioli

Serves 2

You can make this in 30 minutes, but it's better if you let it cook 15 minutes more. It's a big, filling dinner, which you can make even bigger and filling-er by adding bits of ham or thin-sliced dry salami or even a can of clams, but I like it simple and unadorned. If you weren't on a boat, you'd make it with dry beans, soaked overnight and slowly cooked, but there's nothing wrong with canned white beans, well rinsed, if you are on a boat.

If you're rafted up with nice people, this is a good thing to invite them to supper with. Even better next day.

3 Tbsp [45 mL] olive oil
½ cup [125 mL] water
1 large brown onion, chopped fine
3 cloves garlic, chopped fine
1 can [14 oz/398 mL] white beans
1 tsp [5 mL] salt
½ tsp [2 mL] oregano
½ tsp [2 mL] pepper
1 chicken stock cube, dissolved in 1 cup [250 mL] water, *or* 1 cup [250 mL] chicken stock
big handful of dry pasta, something big like penne or macaroni, broken into smallish pieces
1 cup [250 mL] water
chopped parsley for garnish

Heat the olive oil, ½ cup water, onion and garlic in a saucepan. Simmer 3 minutes until the water is almost all gone. Rinse the beans and add to pan with seasonings. Add stock to pan and cook 2 minutes. Stir in pasta and 1 cup water. Cover and simmer 15 minutes, checking occasionally and adding more water as needed. Cook 15–20 minutes more, then drizzle olive oil over top and sprinkle with lots of chopped parsley.

pasta with quick tomato sauce

Serves 4

If you have to be traditional, canned diced tomatoes are your salvation. There's more flesh and less juice than in whole tomatoes, and of course a lot less work and fuss.

spaghetti, linguine, macaroni
    or other pasta for 4
1 medium onion, chopped coarse
2 cloves garlic, chopped fine
2 Tbsp [30 mL] olive oil
¼ cup [60 mL] water
pinch of sugar
1 can [14 oz/398 mL]
    diced tomatoes
1 heaping tsp [7 mL] dried
    oregano, *or* thyme, *or* 1
    tsp [5 mL] rosemary
a few good squirts of tomato
    paste from a tube
juice of half a lemon
lots of fine-chopped parsley

Combine the onion, garlic, olive oil and ¼ cup water in a saucepan. Cook over medium heat until the water is almost all gone. Add sugar, oregano, tomato paste and tomatoes, and cook 20 minutes. Cook pasta al dente. Add lemon juice to sauce, stir well and add parsley. Serve over pasta immediately, sprinkled with grated Parmesan or crumbled feta cheese.

Hint: Pre-grated "Parmesan" cheese doesn't taste very good and doesn't keep. Much better to buy a chunk and grate it yourself. Parmesan in a piece keeps well if tightly wrapped in waxed paper and then sealed in a zip-lock bag.

pasta with black olives

Serves 2
Utterly simple supper.

2 Tbsp [30 mL] olive oil
pinch or two of red pepper flakes
1 small jar black olive
     paste (tapenade)
half a glass of red wine
spaghetti or other pasta for 2
chopped parsley

Cook pasta al dente while you warm the olive oil with the red pepper flakes in a saucepan. Stir in the olive paste and wine, and cook 1 minute. Toss sauce with cooked, drained pasta, sprinkle with parsley and serve.

pasta with baby clams

Serves 2

This couldn't be easier, and it doesn't need cheese.

spaghetti for 2
2 Tbsp [30 mL] olive oil
1 medium onion, chopped
2 cloves garlic, chopped
1 can [10 oz/280 g] baby clams
2 Tbsp [30 mL] tomato paste
½ tsp [2 mL] pepper
salt

Cook pasta al dente. Heat olive oil in a saucepan over medium heat and cook onion and garlic 2 minutes. Add clams, tomato paste and pepper, and check for salt (you may not need it). Pour sauce over cooked pasta.

pasta with peas

Serves 2

Lovely and ridiculously simple—just dry pasta, frozen peas (even canned, if you're desperate) and a can of tuna. If it's springtime and you happen to be tied up near a farmer's market where you can get fresh local peas, then of course forget the frozen.

1 packet [8 oz/225 g] frozen peas
7 oz [200 g] penne *or* other
    large, chunky pasta
3 Tbsp [45 mL] olive oil
2 Tbsp [30 mL] water
1 can [7½ oz/213 g] good tuna
1 tsp [5 mL] dried mint *or*
    a few leaves fresh
½ tsp [2 mL] salt

Tip the peas out onto a plate and separate them a bit so they can start to thaw. Bring a big pot of salted water to the boil and cook the pasta until not quite done, still a bit crunchy. Drain the pasta, but leave it in the pot. Add the peas, olive oil and 2 Tbsp water and cook 2 minutes. Drain off any water that's left, add the tuna and cook 2 minutes, stirring gently. Sprinkle with mint and salt to taste.

penne and potatoes

Serves 4

This is a truly peasant dish—tasty, nourishing and cheap after a hard day's work. The proportions don't matter too much; the potatoes do. Yukon golds are the best; red potatoes are okay (but you have to watch them carefully); russets don't work at all. Penne is the best pasta, but anything chunky–like macaroni–is equally fine.

Try it at home one weekday evening. It's good enough for entertaining, too—just add a green salad and some cheese.

2 Tbsp [30 mL] olive oil
1 medium onion, sliced thin
1 clove garlic, sliced thin
3 medium potatoes, peeled and cut in walnut-sized pieces
½ tsp [2 mL] salt
½ tsp [2 mL] pepper
1 can [14 oz/398 mL] diced tomatoes
½ tsp [2 mL] oregano
½ tsp [2 mL] red pepper flakes
7 oz [200 g] penne *or* other large, chunky pasta
chopped parsley
grated Parmesan and extra olive oil (optional)

Put oil, onions, garlic, potatoes, salt and pepper in a cold fry pan. Stir well, and add enough water to cover the onions by ½" [1 cm]. Cook over medium heat, stirring, until the water is almost gone. Add enough water to cover the potatoes by ¾" [2 cm]. Cover and cook about 10 minutes until potatoes are almost done but still firm. Add tomatoes (with their juice), oregano and red pepper flakes. Bring back to the boil, add the pasta, cover and cook about 10 minutes, until the pasta is cooked but still firm. The pasta should absorb most of the water, and may even need an extra ½ cup [125 mL] or so added to keep it moist. Watch the pan carefully for the last couple of minutes and don't let it stick. Sprinkle chopped parsley over top and sprinkle with grated Parmesan and olive oil.

pasta with eggs
Serves 4

4 eggs
8 oz [250 g] spaghetti *or* linguini
2 Tbsp [30 mL] olive oil
salt and pepper
1 bunch green onions, sliced thin,
    or fresh basil leaves, sliced
2 oz [60 mL] sherry
Parmesan cheese

Crack the eggs into a saucer or cup. Cook the pasta in boiling salted water until almost ready (still a bit crunchy). Remove from heat and drain off all but 1 Tbsp [15 mL] of the water, cover pot and set aside. Heat the oil in a fry pan over medium heat. Slide in the eggs, sprinkle with salt and pepper, cover and cook over medium heat until the whites are set and the yolks are still runny. Put the pasta on plates, slide the eggs on top, garnish with green onion, sprinkle with sherry and grate some Parmesan over top of everything. Eat while it's hot and the yolks are running into the pasta.

instant noodles

Instant noodles are the last resort of the truly unimaginative cook, justified only because they're so quick and so easy. Open the packet, add boiling water, stir and there's a hot meal—soup and noodles. But even on a boat it's hard to justify putting such rubbish into your stomach. The noodles aren't the problem. It's the nasty little "flavour" pack that sometimes comes with them, a combination of dehydrated and virtually nutrition-free ingredients, polysyllabic chemicals, lots of fat and a good dollop of MSG (just to make sure you'll finish up with a headache and a thirst that will wake you at least twice in the night).

But you don't have to buy the whole works. The noodles are available without the nasty little packets. The best ones are what Japanese and Koreans call udon, and Chinese usually call Shanghai-style noodles. Most supermarkets sell them, but for a winter's supply I go to T&T Supermarket and buy a small case of them for less than 50 cents a packet. They're cellophane-wrapped, but it's best to keep them in a screw-top plastic container and yard them out whenever you need a quick supper. They're fat, white and soft, and I've kept packets of them unrefrigerated for 6 months. If you don't want to cook them Asian-style then heat up some tomato sauce in a pan, add a packet of noodles, cover and simmer 2–3 minutes, sprinkle with grated Parmesan cheese and you've made instant spaghetti. Not perfectly Italian spaghetti, but a first-class example of the "make do but make good" style of cooking that gets supper on the table in a hurry.

almost perfect asian-style noodles

Serves 2

This basic recipe works for two people. For four, make it once for two, then rinse out the pan and make it again. At the most it takes 10 minutes, including preparation.

2 Tbsp [30 mL] cooking oil
1 onion, peeled and cut into coarse chunks
¾" [2 cm] piece fresh ginger, sliced as thin as you can
1 clove garlic, crushed
8 oz [250 g] greens (spinach, outside leaves of lettuce, thin-sliced
    cabbage), cut crosswise into 1" [2.5 cm] pieces
2 packets udon noodles
1 Tbsp [15 mL] soy sauce
½ cup [125 mL] water

Heat a fry pan over medium-high heat. Add the cooking oil and stir-fry the onion, ginger and garlic 1 minute. Stir in the greens to coat well with oil. Stir in the noodles, lifting up onions and greens from the bottom. Sprinkle with soy sauce, add water, cover and cook 2–3 minutes. Eat immediately.

Once you've made the basic noodles, you can easily jazz them up next time, with chicken or fish or even a can of salmon. Frozen boneless chicken breasts are available just about everywhere, and so are frozen fish fillets. With a sharp serrated knife, cut either of them into bite-sized pieces while still frozen. Keep the pan on high heat, and after stir-frying the onion, ginger and garlic 1 minute, add the fish or chicken chunks, stir and toss them well for 3 minutes, then add the greens, noodles and water, as in the basic recipe, and cook another 3 minutes. If you are using a can of salmon, add it (juice and all) immediately before adding the noodles and break it up with a fork. A sprinkle of sesame oil (or sesame seeds, or chopped roasted peanuts) gives a great spark to noodles and salmon.

If you're lucky enough to have a fresh fish, I suggest you pan-fry it on its own, sprinkle with a little salt and eat it alongside the basic noodle dish. But a can of shrimp or tuna works well cooked into the basic recipe, and you might try a bit of chopped ham or even garlic sausage. If you're still drinking gin and tonics, and can spare a quick squeeze of lime juice just before you eat, that's nice, but the important thing is to cook it quickly and eat it hot, which is exactly what you need on a September evening as the sun goes down.

winds from the west,
noodles from the east...

tan tan noodles

Serves 2

noodles or spaghetti for 2
1 cup [250 mL] of Super All-
    Purpose Peanut Sauce (p. 28)
½ cup [125 mL] chicken stock
½ tsp [2 mL] red pepper flakes
    or cayenne pepper
chopped cilantro
fine-sliced green onion
handful of roasted peanuts
    (a packet from the
    drugstore is just fine)

Bring a pot of water to a boil, and add noodles or spaghetti. Cook the noodles about 1 minute less than you usually do. (Packaged udon noodles are great for this dish, and they take 2–3 minutes to cook.) Thin out Peanut Sauce with chicken stock, add red pepper flakes or cayenne pepper, and heat until just boiling. Drain the noodles well, add them to the thinned-out sauce, sprinkle with cilantro, green onion and peanuts and serve immediately.

sweet & sour peanut butter noodle soup
Serves 1

The little packages of Asian 3-minute noodles are great emergency rations, as long as you avoid the flavour packet, or modify it: stir 1 tsp [5 mL] Super All-Purpose Peanut Sauce (p. 28) into the soup immediately before serving, and sprinkle with lemon juice. The soup will have a gentle sweet and sour flavour—a considerable improvement on the original.

9 – RICE

Rice is a good thing to have on a boat. It doesn't rot if you keep it in a jar, it's filling, it's easy, leftovers will keep for a day in the icebox and there are dozens of really simple dishes that occur naturally once you stop thinking of rice as something white and tasteless that comes with Chinese food. You can cook it fancy or plain, eat it hot or cold for lunch or dinner, or even breakfast. But you must keep it in a screw-top container. There is something in the genes of mice that leads them directly to rice—down the dock, up the mooring lines, whatever it takes. One friend of mine insists they organize group swims out to boats at anchor. Mice like rice.

The basics are easy. Buy good rice—basmati is the best general-purpose rice, or arborio for fancy dishes, and most supermarkets sell both. Don't buy pre-cooked or instant rice. Despite the ads, they won't save you any time and they taste like cardboard. Put 1 cup [250 mL] of rice, 2 cups [500 mL] of water and a good pinch of salt in a saucepan. Bring to the boil, turn down to simmer, cover and cook 15 minutes. Cook twice as much as you'll eat, and keep leftovers (once they've cooled) in the icebox for tomorrow.

asian almost risotto

Serves 3–4

More fuss is made over risotto than need be. Gourmet magazines go on and on with prissy details, each of which may indeed make a very slight difference to the final product, but the origins of risotto (among other things, Napoleon's chef is supposed to have discovered it on the way to Moscow) are basic peasant, which means supper quick and simple. There's nothing wrong with chicken stock made from a stock cube dissolved in water—you're on a boat.

Almost Risotto is essentially a make-it-up-as-you-go dish—you can add sliced mushrooms with the meat, or chopped sweet red peppers, and you can stir in a handful of chopped greens (lettuce or cabbage leaves) for the last 2 minutes of cooking. Most people call it "Dad's Rice Thing."

2 Tbsp [30 mL] cooking oil
¼ cup [60 mL] water
1 onion, chopped
2 cloves garlic, chopped
10 thin slices fresh ginger
1 tsp [5 mL] pepper
1 cup [250 mL] cubed cooked chicken *or* pork
1 cup [250 mL] rice (not instant)
1 chicken stock cube
2 cups [500 mL] water (or 1 cup/250 mL water, 1 cup/250 mL wine)
soy sauce *or* oyster sauce

Heat oil and water in a fry pan over medium heat. Add onion, garlic, ginger and pepper and cook 4 minutes. Stir in cooked meat and cook 2 minutes. Stir in the rice, mixing well. Dissolve the stock cube in 1 cup [250 mL] of the water and add to rice. Bring to the boil, stir well and add remaining water. Cover and simmer 12 minutes. Turn off heat, let sit 3 minutes, sprinkle with a little soy sauce or oyster sauce and eat.

One of my children uses Spam for meat, which I (on principle) object to, but it's so good I can't turn it down. Just use a bit less soy sauce.

one-pot wonders with rice

Rice takes 15 minutes to cook, which is 15 minutes of steam you can use. Cut some chicken into bite-sized pieces, salt and pepper them well and lay them on the rice as soon as it boils. By the time the rice is cooked, so will the chicken be. Sprinkle it with whatever you have—soy sauce, pasta sauce, tomato paste, peanut sauce. Plain rice needs flavouring, so be generous.

You can also add flavouring to rice while it's cooking. Substitute a can of coconut milk for part of the cooking water, or add a couple of chicken stock cubes. Throw in a handful of chopped roasted almonds and green onions cut into 1" [2.5 cm] pieces and lay them in with the chicken. Halve some cherry tomatoes, toss them with olive oil and lay them on the rice to cook. Dice a couple of slices of ham or break up some canned salmon and let it steam on the rice. Any or all of the extras—even a piece of fresh-caught fish—will cook with the rice. When I steam it this way, I add an extra ½ cup [125 mL] of cooking liquid and let the pot steam for 20 minutes instead of 15.

Breakfast?
Mix 1 cup [250 mL] cold cooked rice with a beaten egg, a pinch of salt and 1 tsp [5 mL] sugar. Heat a fry pan over medium heat, add 1 Tbsp [15 mL] butter or oil, and fry tablespoons of the mixture into little pancakes. Eat them with bacon and/or maple syrup, or sprinkle with sugar and lemon juice.

Lunch?

Start with leftovers—some cold cooked meat and 1 cup [250 mL] cold cooked rice—and make quick-fried rice. Heat 1 Tbsp [15 mL] oil in a fry pan over medium heat. Fry 1 medium onion, chopped fine, 1 carrot, also chopped fine, and ½ tsp [2 mL] pepper for 5 minutes. Stir in the rice to mix everything together. Add 1 cup [250 mL] cold cooked chicken, ham or other cooked meat and whatever flavouring you have (curry powder, thyme, rosemary, chopped garlic). Cook, stirring well, for 10 minutes. Sprinkle with chopped roasted peanuts (straight from the packet is fine) and any green leaves you have (lettuce, cabbage, even dandelion leaves), sliced thin.

Rice salad?

Toss cold cooked rice from yesterday, sliced green onion, chopped green apple (or pear, or peach), salt, pepper, some salad dressing and thin-sliced green leaves. Sprinkle with chopped peanuts, dried coconut or almonds.

Dessert?

Stir some tinned evaporated milk into cold cooked rice, sprinkle with cinnamon and a little sugar, mix with chopped fruit and start your day happy.

10 – DESSERTS

Dessert is the easiest way of turning a simple impromptu meal into what kids call a "proper supper." It has established a reputation as the crowning glory of dinner, the one thing that people will remember, as though dessert had turned into the only valid criterion for judging a cook. So they've become complicated and demanding. Chocolate is essential, whipped cream is almost mandatory and extra points are given for exotic booze and fancy serving dishes. Flames collect a lot of applause in restaurants, but they're about the last thing anybody on a boat needs.

The important thing is that soufflés, baked Alaskas and anything requiring fancy kitchen equipment are not practical. The essence of a good boat dessert is that it is quick and simple. So here's a small collection of easy desserts, most of them based on corner-store ingredients and a lot of them involving no cooking at all.

summer desserts with variations

Ice Cream
In summer there's no problem at all. You can dress up store-bought ice cream with fresh berries and/or plain yogurt and/or a chocolate bar grated over top. If you can pick the berries, even better, and if you can only find them frozen (blueberries, raspberries, strawberries), so be it.

Yogurt
Plain yogurt can be made very attractive by pouring maple syrup or warmed jam or marmalade or honey over top, and/or a sprinkling of chopped nuts or sesame seeds or grated chocolate bars (KitKats grate into an interesting texture). Always buy plain yogurt, then add what you want for dessert. What you don't eat makes a good sauce for a bit of barbecued chicken or salmon.

Apples
One of my favourite desserts has always been a slice of crisp apple and a chunk of good cheddar cheese, but if you insist on sweet things after dinner, then apples will go a long way.

Cut the apples into ½" [1 cm] slices (crosswise or vertically), melt some butter in a fry pan over medium heat, sprinkle the slices with a little sugar and fry them for 5 minutes until lightly browned. Eat them as is, or with yogurt or maple syrup, or slip a spoonful of sherry into the pan and pour the sugary-sherried butter over top, and if you haven't got sherry there's nothing wrong with rye. A spoonful of grated fresh ginger in the butter to start with is nice.

Peaches

Unless peaches are local and fully ripe, they need a little work to make good eating. So treat them the same as apples (p. 106)—slice and fry them in a little butter, with fresh ginger if you've got it. Add a little booze and eat them with yogurt or ice cream. If you've got the barbecue going, cut the peaches in half, take out the stones, lay them on the barbecue cut side up, put a little sugar and butter in the holes where the stones were, lay a piece of foil loosely over top and grill for 5–6 minutes.

Pears

Most pears in corner stores and marinas are either unripe or overripe. Don't bother with the overripe, which you can recognize. The unripe can be easily cooked. Cut the pears in half vertically and put them in a small saucepan with enough red wine to cover, 2 Tbsp [30 mL] sugar and ½ tsp [2 mL] rosemary or thyme. Simmer over low heat for 10–15 minutes while you eat your main course. Eat hot or cold with (you know now) ice cream or yogurt or chocolate bars, and eat the leftovers next day, sprinkled with a little vinegar as a chutney side dish for your cold meat.

Bananas

You can fry sliced banana in butter and booze (follow the directions under Peaches and Apples, above), but be careful not to overcook them—about 2 minutes is the maximum.

barbecued bananas

All banana desserts are just plain lovely. The simplest of all is barbecued.

Lay whole unpeeled bananas on the barbecue over medium heat and cook about 10 minutes turning after 5. The skin will go brown. Slide the bananas onto a plate, slit the skin the length of the banana with a sharp knife and open it out a bit. Put in a knob of butter and some brown sugar, or some yogurt or ice cream or canned milk. Spoon the bananas out of their skins, all buttery and sticky. Eat them right away.

banana omelette

Serves 2

If you want to impress or seduce someone, or blackmail your children into being very, very good, this is the answer. It's a little work but worth it. Serve it for breakfast or dessert.

2 Tbsp [30 mL] butter
2 bananas, peeled and sliced
5 eggs
½ tsp [2 mL] salt
apricot jam *or* marmalade

Heat the butter in a fry pan over medium heat and fry the banana slices in butter until lightly caramelized on both sides. Meanwhile, vigorously beat the eggs and salt with 2 half-eggshells of cold water. Push the bananas to the centre of the pan and add the eggs. Cover and cook 4–5 minutes, until the top is just set. Spoon directly out of the pan onto plates, and drizzle jam over top.

sweet omelette

Serves 2

This is a quick, lovely, fast dessert that you can make after your main course. It's a nice thing to make for a birthday or another seduction.

4 eggs, separated
2 Tbsp [30 mL] sugar
pinch salt
2 Tbsp [30 mL] butter

Beat the egg whites as stiff as you can with 1 or 2 forks, slowly adding 1 Tbsp of the sugar as you beat. Beat the yolks with the same fork(s), adding the rest of the sugar and the salt, until they're smooth and yellow. Heat the butter in a fry pan over medium-low heat until bubbling. Fold the egg yolks into the whites and pour immediately into the pan. Cover and cook 2–3 minutes. Uncover, turn up heat and finish with 1 minute of cooking to lightly brown the bottom. The omelette will rise and become puffy. Sprinkle with a bit of sugar or syrup or Smarties or chocolate chips. Happy whatever.

corn fritters

Serves 2

These fritters are more a variation on pancakes, and they're perfectly fine made with fresh, frozen or canned corn. They are very good indeed anytime, including breakfast time. The fritters need baking powder, which tends to lose its fizz on boats, so just buy a small can of it and test it before using. How to test? Drop ½ tsp [2 mL] into a glass of cold water. If it fizzes, it's fine. If it doesn't, chuck it out and make something else for dessert.

**1 cob fresh corn *or* 1 cup [250 mL]
    frozen *or* canned (drained)
    whole-kernel corn
2 Tbsp [30 mL] flour
2 eggs
1 tsp [5 mL] baking powder
1 Tbsp [15 mL] sugar
½ tsp [2 mL] salt
butter and/or oil for frying**

Cut the kernels off the cob. Mix the corn well with the flour, eggs, baking powder, sugar and salt. Fry spoonfuls of the batter in butter or oil for a few minutes until well browned on both sides. Eat with maple syrup and/or yogurt or fruit—or, best of all, with maple syrup and slices of crisp bacon.

country bougatsa

Serves 2

Pita bread is a good thing for weekends on boats—it stays fresh in the packet and goes with just about anything. You need a small leap of the imagination to turn it into bougatsa, but that's what it was called when I first ate it in Greece, and if you've got the barbecue going, you should try it.

1 pita
2 heaping Tbsp [35 mL]
   crumbled feta cheese
big pinch of oregano
2 Tbsp [30 mL] liquid honey
   (or maple syrup)

Cut a pita bread in half, and carefully open the pockets. Poke remaining ingredients into each pocket. Squeeze the edges of the pita together, and lay it on the grill over medium heat. Cook 2–3 minutes on each side, until the pita is a bit crisped and the cheese has just melted. Eat them as they come off the grill.

jam butties

Serves 1

In some parts of England they eat chip butties—French fries inside, instead of jam.

2 slices bread
butter
jam
1 egg
1 Tbsp [15 mL] sugar plus
    extra for sprinkling

One jam butty starts with 2 slices of bread, both buttered and one generously spread with jam, then put together. Now beat egg in a bowl with sugar. Heat butter in a fry pan over medium heat. Dip the butty in the egg on both sides (squish it a bit) and fry it in the pan until both sides are brown. Sprinkle with sugar and serve with yogurt.

oranges for adults

If you slice an unpeeled orange very thin indeed (a serrated bread knife is best), then arrange the slices overlapping on a plate, sprinkle with sugar and rye (or tequila, or sherry) and then let it sit and marinate for 30 minutes you will have a very pleasant ending to your dinner.

11 – ONE-POT CHRISTMAS

Christmas on a boat can be a wonderful experience, or it can be a horror show. I've had both. Which one you get seems to have nothing to do with weather—rain and snow are just other dimensions, other colours in the palette of memory—and Santa isn't important. Everybody knows that you just can't get a new Mercedes down the chimney. Dragging anchor at 3:00 a.m., falling off the bow while leaving the dock, having to dismantle the head—I've done them all on different Christmas mornings, with different soulmates, and we're still friends. But the holiday I never want to repeat was with somebody who just couldn't accept that the most important thing about Christmas on a boat is simply remembering *that it's on a boat,* and the rules are different.

Parties were planned, people were to be met and picked up from docks, dinner (for 8) had to be turkey, red wine couldn't possibly go in the same glass as white, and "You can't have dinner in that shirt ... " Love disappeared, then affection, and finally civility. We were sailing a 45-footer, but that was the year I decided no boat was big enough for more than two people to live on, certainly not at Christmas.

But at Christmas, dockside or at anchor, it's always serenely quiet because very few people go out for the holiday. There always seem to be lots of herons and lots of otters, and sticking your head out of the hatch while the coffee brews makes for wonderful mornings. Mid-winter guarantees success with the crab trap, and a couple of cedar branches make for decoration. Coffee and presents in bed, the new CD, tangerines for breakfast, a quick check on the weather, maybe champagne and maybe you don't get up until noon.

christmas cornish game hens

Serves 2

Sometime during the day you have to have Christmas dinner, and it's nice if it has a wishbone. Even nicer if you don't have to clean the oven. Cornish game hens are my favourite holiday main course. Most supermarkets sell them frozen. They keep for a couple of days in an ordinary icebox, defrost in 3–4 hours when you take them out, and cook in just over an hour even if they're not fully defrosted when you start.

The trick is to cook them on top of the stove, in a rich tomato sauce. The whole dinner goes in one pot—vegetables, potatoes, bird (or birds). Despite the apparent simplicity of this dinner it's undeniably festive, smells wonderful and is virtually fuss-free. You need the big 5 qt [5 L] pot that even the smallest boat should have (for cooking crabs, soaking your feet, bailing, cooking pasta, bathing the cat). I like to cook crab in the pot for an appetizer (see p. 59), empty the pot, rinse it out, and it's ready for cooking dinner.

2 Tbsp [30 mL] olive oil
1 Cornish game hen, defrosted
2 medium onions, peeled and left whole
1 clove garlic, chopped
3 medium potatoes, quartered lengthwise
1 can [19 oz/540 mL] diced tomatoes with red peppers
large glass of red wine
salt and pepper

Heat the pot, add the oil, wipe the game hen dry and brown it a bit over medium-high heat for 5 minutes. Add the onions, garlic and potatoes and toss to coat with oil. Add the tomatoes, stir and bring to the boil. Add the wine, salt and pepper, turn the bird in the sauce, turn the heat to low, cover and let cook for an hour, spooning the sauce over the bird every 15 minutes. If the sauce looks as if it's going to stick, add more wine. Shuck the crab for an appetizer, light a candle, sing carols, drink the rest of the wine and enjoy the smells coming from the stove.

If there are leftovers, boil them up next day with a chopped onion and a bit more red wine, and you have a quick Boxing Day pasta sauce.

cheater's trifle

For each dessert: 1 slice of any store-bought plain cake (lemon cake, sponge cake) in the bottom of a bowl, 2–3 Tbsp [30–45 mL] frozen raspberries on top, 1 tsp [5 mL] sherry (or brandy or whatever booze you have) on the raspberries, and a big heaping dollop of plain yogurt on top of everything, Let it sit while you eat the game hen. More carols, more wine, very few dishes, check the weather, blow out the candle and back to bed.

And that's it—dinner's ready, a rich and flavourful Christmas meal.

INDEX

African chicken stew, 40

almost perfect Asian-style noodles, 96

appetizers, 7–16

apples: 106; pork chops and, 49

Asian almost risotto, 101

asparagus, grilled, 75

bacon salad, hot, 20

baked olives, 8

banana: barbecued, 108; fried, 107; omelette, 109

barbecue: 71–77; bananas, 108; cedar-barbecued salmon, 74; flank steak, 72; pork chops for two, 73; vegetables, 75–76

basic quick peanut sauce, 29; 77

basic salad dressing, 18

basil, 6

bbq pork chops for two, 73

beach oysters, 63

bouillabaisse, 57

cabbage: 78–82; 101, 79; 201, 80; 301, 81; salad, 22; spicy, 82

canned food: clams, 4; consommé, 4; corn, 4; salmon, 4, 66–70; tomatoes, 4

carrots, grilled, 76

cedar-barbecued salmon, 74

cheater's trifle, 117

chicken: and grapes, 43; and oranges, 46; and peanuts, 41; and rye, 42; biryani, 44; on the grill, 73; stew, African, 40; 25-minute with tomatoes and ginger, 47

chickpea vinaigrette, 15

chowder, salmon, 68

Christmas: Cornish game hens, 116; one-pot, 115

clams: or mussels, plain or fancy, 60; canned, 84; Daniel, 12; with pasta, 90

corned beef hash, 51

corn: fritters, 111; grilled on the cob, 76

country bougatsa, 112

crab, fresh, 59

dessert: 105–114; summer variations, 106–107

don't ask, don't tell quick pasta, 85

dressing, salad 6, 18

egg(s): 31–38; au naturel, 38; banana omelette, 109; benedict with variations, 37; huevos rancheros, boat style, 33; mayonnaise, 6; omelette, 35; salad, 6;

egg(s) continued: salad, Russian, 9;
scrambled à deux, 36; sweet
omelette, 110; tortilla española, 32;
with pasta, 94

equipment, 2–3

fagioli fiorentina, 25
fancy oyster stew, 64
fennel salad, 19
fishcakes, 4, 70
fish with peanut butter sauce, 58
foil-packet dinners, 77

garlic: bread, grilled 71;
mushrooms, 11
ginger: 4, 5; 52–53; tea, 54
green beans, grilled, 75
green peas, grilled, 76
grilled garlic bread, 71
grilled vegetables, 75-76

herbs and spices, 5–6
hot bacon salad, 20
hot salad of sweet peppers, 23
huevos rancheros, boat style, 33

ice-cream, 106
instant noodles, 95-99

jam butties, 113

lettuce: grilled, 75; radicchio, 75;
romaine, 75

matelote de fevrier, or my Aunt Sallie's
cheapo 20-minute bouillabaisse, 57
mayonnaise, eggy, 6
meat and poultry, 39-51
mint: and mushrooms, 13; and
mushrooms and tuna, 14
mushroom(s): garlic, 11; and mint, 13; and
mint and tuna, 14; salad with green

beans, warm, 24
mussels, plain or fancy clams or, 60

noodles 95-99: almost perfect asian-style,
96; instant, 95; tan tan, 98

oils, 4, 18
olives, baked, 8
olive oil and pasta, 84
omelette: 35; banana, 109; sweet, 110
one-pot Christmas, 115-117
one-pot wonders with rice, 103
oranges for adults, 114
oysters, beach, 63
oyster stew, fancy, 64

pappa al pomodoro, 48
pasta 83-94: and noodles, 83; and olive
oil, 84; don't ask, don't tell quick, 85;
fagioli, 86; penne and potatoes, 92;
with baby clams, 90;

pasta continued: with black olives, 89; with eggs, 94; with peas, 91; with quick tomato sauce, 88

peaches, 107

peanut butter: 4; 27; 30; noodle soup, sweet & sour, 99; salad, 26; sauce with fish, 58

peanuts: and chicken, 41; spiced, 16; spicy pork chops, 50

peanut sauce: basic quick, 29, 77; super all-purpose, 28

pears, 107

peas: grilled, 76; with pasta, 91

penne and potatoes, 92

plain or fancy clams or mussels, 60

pink salmon, 61

potatoes: grilled, 76; penne and, 92; salmon salad, 67; with walnuts and yogurt, 10

pork chops: and apples, 49; bbq for two, 73; spicy peanut, 50

rice: 4, 100-104; one pot wonders, 103; salad, 104

risotto, Asian almost, 101

Russian egg salad, 9

salad: 17-26; 62; basic dressing, 18; cabbage, 22; fennel, 19; hot bacon, 20; peanut butter, 26; rice 104; Russian egg, 9; salmon potato, 67; sweet peppers, hot, 23; warm mushroom with green beans, 24

salmon: 66-70; canned, 4; cedar-barbecued, 74; chowder, 68; fishcakes, 70; pink, 61; potato salad, 67; sandwiches, 66; sesame stir-fry, 69

scrambled eggs à deux, 36

seafood, fresh, 55-65

sesame salmon stir-fry, 69

shio yaki, 56

spaghetti, 85

spiced peanuts, 16

spicy cabbage, 82

spicy peanut pork chops (or chicken breast), 50

summer desserts with variations, 106–107

super all-purpose peanut sauce, 28

sweet omelet, 110

sweet peppers: grilled, 75; hot salad, 23

sweet & sour peanut butter noodle soup, 99

tan tan noodles, 98

tortilla española, 32

trifle, cheater's, 117

tuna, mushrooms and mint, 14

vinaigrette, chickpea, 15

warm mushroom salad with green beans, 24